Praise for Robert Kagan's

THE JUNGLE GROWS BACK

"It is time to say it: I am a Kaganite. . . . There is no modern author who has taught me more, or changed the way I view the world more, than he has. . . . For identifying and clearly explaining the chief forces driving human history, Bob is brilliant."   —Michael E. O'Hanlon,
Brookings Institution

"[Kagan] has in many ways become the biographer of American power. . . . He brings to the page a true sense of the stakes involved—not some abstract notion of the 'rules-based order,' but the basic security and prosperity of Americans."   —*Commentary*

"*The Jungle Grows Back* displays the characteristic Kagan virtues of lucid writing and thought—and a strong sense of history that adds drama and sweep to his argument."
—Gideon Rachman, *Financial Times*

"This short book is a valuable read and makes a valiant effort to argue for America's continued deep engagement in the world. . . . The world order is not natural; it needed to be built and it needs to be carefully maintained."
—Doug Stokes, *Quillette*

"[Robert] Kagan has a new book, *The Jungle Grows Back*, part elegy, part alarum about the United States as part of the problem. Rattled allies are on his side—and saying so. So should Americans of all stripes." —Strobe Talbott

"A provocative argument that runs counter to popular sentiment and conventional wisdom." —*Kirkus Reviews*

"An eye-opening assessment." —*Booklist*

ROBERT KAGAN

THE JUNGLE GROWS BACK

Robert Kagan is a senior fellow at the Brookings Institution and a columnist for *The Washington Post*. He is also the author of *The Return of History and the End of Dreams, Dangerous Nation, Of Paradise and Power*, and *A Twilight Struggle*. He served in the U.S. State Department from 1984 to 1988. He lives in Virginia with his wife.

THE JUNGLE
GROWS BACK

THE JUNGLE
GROWS BACK

America and Our Imperiled World

ROBERT KAGAN

VINTAGE BOOKS
A Division of Penguin Random House LLC
New York

FIRST VINTAGE BOOKS EDITION, AUGUST 2019

Copyright © 2018 by Robert Kagan

The Library of Congress has cataloged the Knopf edition as follows:
Names: Kagan, Robert, author.
Title: The jungle grows back : America and our imperiled world /
Robert Kagan.
Description: First edition. | New York : Alfred A. Knopf, 2018.
Identifiers: LCCN 2018011882 (print) | LCCN 2018013593 (ebook)
Subjects: LCSH: World politics—1945–1989. | World politics—1989– |
Security, International. | United States—Foreign relations—1945–1989. |
United States—Foreign relations—1989– | BISAC: HISTORY / United
States / 20th Century. | POLITICAL SCIENCE / International Relations /
General. | HISTORY / Modern / General.
Classification: LCC E744 (ebook) | LCC E744 .K147 2018 (print) |
DDC 327.73009/04—dc23
LC record available at https://lccn.loc.gov/2018011882

Vintage Books Trade Paperback ISBN: 978-0-525-56357-0
eBook ISBN: 978-0-525-52166-2

Author photograph © Cyndy Porter
Book design by Maggie Hinders

www.vintagebooks.com

Printed in the United States of America
10 9 8 7 6 5 4 3

For Dad

THE JUNGLE
GROWS BACK

THE AMERICAN-LED LIBERAL WORLD ORDER was never a natural phenomenon. It was not the culmination of evolutionary processes across the millennia or the inevitable fulfillment of universal human desires. The past seven-plus decades of relatively free trade, growing respect for individual rights, and relatively peaceful cooperation among nations—the core elements of the liberal order—have been a great historical aberration. Until 1945 the story of humankind going back thousands of years was a long tale of war, tyranny, and poverty. Moments of peace were fleeting, democracy so rare as to seem almost accidental, and prosperity the luxury of the powerful few. Our own era has not lacked its horrors, its genocides, its oppressions, its barbarisms. Yet by historical standards, including the standards of the recent past, it has been a relative paradise. Between 1500 and 1945 scarcely a year passed when the strongest powers in the world, the great powers of Europe, were not at war, but since 1945 there have been no wars among the great powers.[1] The great Cold War confrontation between the United States and the Soviet Union ended peacefully, a historical rarity. Meanwhile, deaths from all recent smaller wars have declined dramatically, as indeed have violent deaths of all kinds. Since the end of the Second World War the world has also enjoyed a period of prosperity unlike any other, with more than seven decades of global GDP growth averaging almost 3.5 percent per year, despite the 2007–2008 financial crisis. Since 1945, some four billion people around the world have climbed out of poverty. The number of democratic governments has grown from no more than a dozen in 1939 to more than a hundred today. The power of the state has been curbed in favor of the individual in large parts of the world, and an ever-expanding panoply of individual rights has come to be respected. What Abraham Lincoln called the "better angels" of human nature have been encouraged, and some of human beings' worst impulses have been suppressed more effectively than before.[2] But all this has been an anomaly in the history of human existence. The liberal world order is fragile and impermanent. Like a garden, it is ever under siege from the natural forces of history, the jungle whose vines and weeds constantly threaten to overwhelm it.

Unfortunately, we tend to take our world for granted. We have lived so long inside the bubble of the liberal order that we can imagine no other kind of world. We think it is natural and normal, even inevitable. We see all its flaws and wish it could be better, but it doesn't occur to us that the more likely alternative to it would be much, much worse. Unlike other cultures, which view history as a continuous cycle of growth and decay, or as stasis, we view history as having a direction and a purpose. We believe in "modernization," in stages of economic and political development, in the link between prosperity and democracy. As children of the Enlightenment, we believe the expansion of knowledge and material progress goes hand in hand with improvements in human behavior and moral progress. From Montesquieu and Kant we learned that commerce tames the souls of men and nations, reducing conflict and increasing harmony and cooperation. From Marx and others we learned to treat stages of economic development as the drivers of political development—feudalism produces government by monarchs and aristocrats, capitalism produces government by parliaments and democracies, all as part of some iron logic of economic determinism. From Hegel we learned that history is but "the progress of the consciousness of freedom" and that, as Francis Fukuyama put it in his famous description of the "End of History," there is "a common evolutionary pattern for all societies . . . something like a Universal History of mankind in the direction of liberal democracy."[3] Hence we have come to believe that, while there may be occasional bumps and detours on the road, progress is inevitable.

This story of human progress is a myth, however. If the last century has taught us anything, it is that scientific and technological progress and the expansion of knowledge, while capable of improving our lives materially, have brought no lasting improvement in human behavior. Nor is history rightly viewed as a progressive upward march toward enlightenment. That perception rests on a carefully curated set of facts. We jump from Periclean Athens to the birth of Christianity, from the Renaissance to the Reformation, from the Magna Carta to the American Revolution. Omitted from this tale of golden ages and great leaps forward are the dark ages and great leaps backward. When it comes to human behavior, history is a jagged line with no discernible slope. Where on the scale of progress would we put the Thirty Years' War, which killed off almost half the populations of the German principalities, or the Napoleonic Wars, which killed more than three million Europeans, destroyed the lives of many millions more, and helped produce the revolutionary nationalism that would wreak so much havoc in the first decades of the twentieth century? How do World War I, World War II, the famines, and the genocides of the last century fit into our story of human progress? Were the horrors perpetrated against Ukrainians and Chinese in the 1930s and against Jews in the 1940s part of our story of progress? Were they just aberrations, or were they harbingers of the future? Only by ignoring much horrendous bloodshed and brutality, and quite recently in historical terms, can we believe that there has been anything like a steady improvement in the way humans treat each other.

Nor has there been steady progress toward liberalism. Liberal government flickered into existence at the end of the eighteenth century, first in Great Britain and America and then, inspired by the French Revolution, in parts of Europe in the nineteenth and twentieth centuries. But as liberalism grew, so did the modern police state, which was born in Austria, Prussia, and Russia at the end of the eighteenth century and was gradually perfected in the nineteenth and twentieth. (And the French Revolution did not produce liberalism in France before going through stages of totalitarianism followed by strongman rule.) Stirrings of liberalism in nineteenth-century Germany, Italy, and Poland were repeatedly crushed by absolutist powers using force, repression, and censorship. A brief flowering of democratic government after World War I was quickly extinguished and supplanted by the rise of fascism and communism. If the Second World War had produced a different set of victors, as it might have, liberalism might not have survived the twentieth century outside of North America.

Few in the middle of the last century saw liberalism on the rise. A survey of the world in 1939 would not have suggested to anyone that history was pointing toward a triumph of the liberal idea. "I am . . . a bear on democracy," Joseph Kennedy told Walter Lippmann in London that year. "It's gone already."[4] As Hannah Arendt put it, writing in 1950, to view Western Civilization as a steady march of progress was to ignore the "subterranean stream of Western history."[5] History had not led to the triumph of liberalism; it had led to Hitler and Stalin. Throughout the Cold War, which seemed as if it would last forever, there was little reason to regard history as a steady progression toward a better world. The political theorist Judith Shklar, writing in the late 1950s, observed that in an age of two world wars, totalitarianism, and mass murder, "no reasonable person" could "believe in any 'law' of progress."[6] After witnessing humanity at its worst, Arendt insisted, "we can no longer afford to take that which was good in the past and simply call it our heritage, to discard the bad and simply think of it as a heavy load which by itself time will bury in oblivion."[7]

But apparently we can. Among the worst horrors of recorded history occurred in the lifetimes of our grandparents. Just seventy-five years ago Hitler was rampaging across Europe, Stalin was starving millions through forced collectivization, Japanese soldiers were raping and killing in Nanjing, millions were systematically being put to death in gas chambers in Eastern and Central Europe, and the United States was dropping nuclear bombs on Japanese cities. Yet after a few remarkable decades of relative peace, prosperity, and democracy, many became convinced that the human race had changed fundamentally, that after millennia of war, poverty, and tyranny, of individual and collective brutality, of tribalism and racism, human beings had over the course of a few decades suddenly become less violent, less warlike, more caring, more open. Some international relations theorists continue to believe that "the grand mechanism for overturning old international orders—great power war—has disappeared"; law professors argue that the very "nature of conflict" among nations "has changed fundamentally" (because of the Kellogg-Briand Pact of 1928 "outlawing war"); the cognitive psychologist Steven Pinker, who documents the decline of violence in the world since 1945, argues that the reason this happened in such a "short span of time was that the arguments that slew them belong to a coherent philosophy that emerged during the Age of Reason and the Enlightenment."[8] Perhaps fewer people today believe that the "liberal idea," all but extinguished in the 1930s, won an irreversible victory after the collapse of Soviet communism, now that authoritarianism is enjoying a renaissance. But many continue to assume that, even so, our dark recent past is indeed in the past and cannot recur.

Here is an alternative hypothesis. We have witnessed amazing progress over the past seven decades, and not just technological progress but also human progress. Yet this progress was not the culmination of anything. It was not the product of evolution, of expanding knowledge, of technological advances, the spread of commerce, and least of all of any change in the basic nature of human beings. It has been the product of a unique set of circumstances contingent on a particular set of historical outcomes, including on the battlefield, that could have turned out differently. It has been, above all, the by-product of a new configuration of power in the international system, the rise to preeminence of a new player on the international scene with a unique and advantageous geography, a large and productive population, unprecedented economic and military power, and, as it happened, a national ideology based on the liberal principles of the Enlightenment. The present world order has favored liberalism, democracy, and capitalism not only because they are right and better— presumably they were right and better in the 1930s, too—but because the most powerful nation in the world since 1945 has been a liberal democratic capitalist nation. That, too, was not fated but was the consequence of unique circumstances and contingent historical events. After World War II, because of America's unrivaled power, those Enlightenment principles suddenly enjoyed a force behind them that they had never before possessed. What we liberals call progress has been made possible by the protection afforded liberalism within the geographical and geopolitical space created by American power. This was not the inevitable unfolding of some Universal History. On the contrary, the creation of the liberal order has been an act of defiance against both history and human nature.

People today ask what threatens the present order, but that is the wrong question. The order is an artificial creation subject to the forces of geopolitical inertia. Deeply etched patterns of history, interrupted these past seven decades, remain and exert their pull. The question is not what will bring down the liberal order but what can possibly hold it up? If the liberal order is like a garden, artificial and forever threatened by the forces of nature, preserving it requires a persistent, unending struggle against the vines and weeds that are constantly working to undermine it from within and overwhelm it from without.

Today there are signs all around us that the jungle is growing back. Where once many hoped that all the nations and peoples of the world would converge on a common path of liberal democratic capitalist development, we now see authoritarianism surviving if not thriving. Today a Russian dictator and European would-be dictators boast of their illiberalism, and a Chinese leader, wielding the absolute power of a Mao, portrays his nation as a model for the world. Where once we believed that economic success must eventually require political liberalization, we now see autocracies successfully practicing a state capitalism compatible with repressive government. Where once many believed geo-economics had replaced geopolitics, today we see the world returning to a geopolitics much like that of the late nineteenth and twentieth centuries. Territorial aggression, once thought to be an anachronism, has returned to Europe and threatens to return to Asia. Where once people believed that the nation-state was a thing of the past in an increasingly cosmopolitan and interconnected age, we now see nationalism and tribalism reemerging, more than able to hold their own in the brave new world of the Internet. Meanwhile, a profound and extended crisis of confidence besets the democratic world, even in the birthplace of modern democracy. Liberal international institutions like the European Union, once considered the vanguard of a postmodern future, are now under assault from without and within. In America, racial and tribal forces that have always been part of the "subterranean stream" of American history have reemerged to reshape politics and society. Where thirty years ago the dreams of Enlightenment thinkers going back three centuries seemed to be on the cusp of fulfillment, today a Counter-Enlightenment of surprising potency stirs in Moscow, Budapest, Beijing, Tehran, and Cairo, in parts of Western Europe, and even in the nation that saved liberalism seventy-five years ago.

In the face of this unanticipated shift in direction, our excessive optimism has turned to excessive pessimism. Less than three decades ago we were told that the triumph of liberalism was inevitable; today we read that liberalism's failure is inevitable. One fatalistic determinism has replaced another.

As the liberal order confronts multiplying crises from both within and without, Americans and their political leaders have not responded as they might have in the past. There is no call to action to reverse the trends. Some still hold to the old optimistic assumptions, as if nothing has happened to make us doubt their validity. Even some of our best-informed experts still believe China must eventually open its political system, notwithstanding China's determined move in the opposite direction; that Russia cannot continue on its current political and geopolitical trajectory without collapsing economically, despite two decades of evidence to the contrary; or that in Europe liberal ideals are so deeply implanted that they can never be uprooted. Many still regard peace as the norm and war the aberration, something that occurs only by accident or miscalculation. They still see the world through the distorting lens of the liberal order's bubble. For some, belief in the End of History dies hard.

More pervasive these days, however, is a profound skepticism about the liberal order's durability and even its desirability. An increasing number on both the left and the right have come to regard the struggle to uphold the order as either hopeless or mistaken. Self-described "realists" insist that Americans must learn to accept the world as it is, not as we would wish it to be. Decrying the "failures and follies" of the past quarter century—the wars in Iraq and Afghanistan, the interventions of the 1990s, the expansion of NATO, which they regard as a mistake, and the broader effort to support democracy in allegedly inhospitable places—they call for a new policy of "restraint."[9] American policies in support of a liberal world order have not only overtaxed and exhausted Americans, they argue, but have done no good for them or for others. In 2011 Barack Obama, in announcing a drawdown of U.S. troops in Afghanistan, argued that it was "time to focus on nation building here at home."[10] Five years later Donald Trump echoed the sentiment, telling voters that the liberal order was a bad deal and it was time to put "America First."

Polls show that Americans mostly agree. In 2016, 57 percent of Americans polled believed the U.S. should "mind its own business" and let the rest of the world manage its own problems, up from just 30 percent a decade and a half earlier. When Americans elected Trump, 41 percent believed the United States was "doing too much" in the world, and only 27 percent believed it was not doing enough.[11] This mood did not begin with Trump, or even with Obama. The 2016 election was the fourth presidential contest since the race between George W. Bush and Al Gore in 2000 in which the candidate promising to pursue a narrower definition of American interests and to reduce American involvement overseas defeated candidates in the primaries and in the general election who stood for a more expansive foreign policy. The public desire for a reduction of overseas involvement has been growing for three decades. It preceded the Iraq War and the war in Afghanistan, and it persisted despite the events of September 11, 2001, the worst attack on American soil since Pearl Harbor, the continuing threat of radical Islamic terrorism, and the growing threats that Americans perceive from North Korea, Iran, China, and Russia. Today Americans question why their nation has to be so deeply involved in the rest of the world, why they have to spend lives and money on such apparently hopeless places as the Middle East, why rich allies like Germany, Japan, and South Korea cannot take care of themselves, and why the United States must risk war for matters that seem at a remove from America's immediate economic and security interests.

These are reasonable questions, and it is wrong to refer to those who ask them as "isolationists." Few are suggesting that the United States pull up the drawbridge and cut off all ties with the outside world. What most critics and skeptics of American foreign policy today want is for the United States to act more like a normal nation. And it is true that for more than seven decades the United States has not been acting like a "normal" country. No nation in history has ever been more deeply involved in the affairs of the world nor accepted more responsibility for the state of humankind than the United States since the Second World War. Very few nations in history have ever felt any responsibility for anything but themselves. The vast majority of nations do not think twice about looking after their own narrow interests "first." Americans have been abnormal in this respect—abnormal in their willingness to shoulder great moral and material burdens in order to preserve this abnormal liberal order. To question whether they must continue to do so, to ask whether the benefits still outweigh the costs, is not "isolationist." It is natural.

So how to answer the many Americans who are skeptical of the benefits of such extensive global involvement? One can try to point out that the costs and risks of not continuing to play this role will be much higher, but that is a hard thing to prove before events take their course. Americans see the costs of upholding this order; the costs of not upholding it are unknown. We can see the risks of taking action; the risks of inaction are harder to predict. Perhaps the best we can do is look to our past for guidance.

RETURN TO THE 1930S

This is not the first time Americans have asked these kinds of questions, after all. Although we tend to take American foreign policy during the Cold War as the norm against which to measure American attitudes toward the world today, that is a misleading basis for comparison. The Cold War was an unusual period in American history, a time when many Americans, for a variety of reasons, were persuaded that deep and extensive global involvement was essential to preserving American interests. That was never the American view before the Cold War, and it is not the view today.

The questions Americans are posing today are actually much more like those posed in the twenty years after the First World War. The 1920s and 1930s were a time when, like today, most Americans did not believe they faced an existential threat to their security and way of life, when threats were visible but uncertain, when Americans were weary and disillusioned by a recent war. The United States was not the only great power in the world, even though it was the richest and for a time the strongest. Great Britain had taken responsibility for sustaining some semblance of world order for the past century, and so it still seemed plausible to let Britain and the other great powers continue taking responsibility for the world's problems while Americans looked after "America First," as Warren Harding proposed in his presidential campaign in 1920. He called then, as many call now, for a "return to normalcy."

Their story is worth recalling, for it was they who eventually abandoned normalcy and created the order the United States has been upholding ever since the end of the Second World War. The generations of the interwar period had not started out with that in mind—in fact, they did all they could to avoid it. As a result, they have a reputation for having been "isolationists," blind to the dangers that we today can see were lying ahead of them. This is an unfair and smug perspective. Those Americans were not so different from us. We can learn much from their experience.

They, too, began a new century optimistic about the future of humankind. Before World War I, after decades of peace, the transatlantic world at the dawn of the new century enjoyed an unprecedented prosperity, with an increasingly global economy and revolutions in communication and transportation that were bringing peoples and nations closer. The number of democracies in the world had grown from five to ten, and many believed that "the idea of popular government" had become "so universal" that there could no longer be any doubt of its "final triumph," as the great populist and Democratic Party leader William Jennings Bryan put it.[12] They shared our view of progress, believing that all of history was an upward climb from ignorance and barbarism to understanding and civilization and that the end point was liberalism and peace. Even Theodore Roosevelt at the turn of the century believed war between the "civilized" powers was likely a thing of the past. He and others feared only that the world's backward peoples, the "barbarians" in Asia, Africa, and the Middle East, would bring the world to ruin if they were not checked and taught the ways of civilized existence through commerce and wise guidance from the more advanced nations. As the British author and politician Norman Angell observed in 1909, the world's great, civilized powers, had "passed out of that stage of development" in which any nation could benefit from conquering another by force.[13] Reasoned calculations of self-interest precluded war among them. In a world of growing prosperity, democracy, and increasing connection among peoples, great-power war was obsolete.

It turned out that they were no better at predicting the future than we are (and also no worse). They did not foresee that the deadliest challenge to Western Civilization would come a mere five years after Angell wrote those words, and not from the Middle East, or Africa, or Asia, but from a great and horrifically destructive war in the very heart of that civilization between nations that were the home of Goethe and Mozart and of Rousseau and Voltaire. They could not imagine that the world's leading commercial powers, so interdependent in the modern global economy, would wage a war for such primitive goals as territory and military domination, that they would be inspired not by rational calculations of interest but by fear, pride, and ambition, and that war would enjoy the enthusiastic backing of their people fueled by nationalism and tribalism. They did not anticipate a rebellion against liberalism, from the right in the form of a German ruling class defending the all-powerful state, and from the left in the form of a Bolshevism rejecting the liberal principles of private property and individual rights. Then, every one of their assumptions about the modern world exploded at once.

Americans at first watched the war in Europe that erupted in 1914 as if it were a distant explosion—frightening, fascinating, far away, and, most thought, none of their business. They quickly discovered to their surprise that their economy, though hardly dependent on international trade, was nevertheless tightly intertwined with that of the Europeans. They grew rich from the war but also unwittingly became a critical factor in the struggle, such that they were eventually drawn into it by the participants on both sides. They were drawn in not only to protect their trade and neutral rights, however, but also to defend what Walter Lippmann at the time called the "Atlantic community," the collection of liberal and democratic nations on both shores of the Atlantic with whom the United States shared not only economic interests but also a common political and moral worldview.[14]

The important ideological aspects of the First World War have been obscured or dismissed by generations of historians and political scientists. We have been taught to smirk at Woodrow Wilson's appeal to "make the world safe for democracy." But as the German historian Wolfgang J. Mommsen once observed, the war was, in fact, not just "a struggle for power among the nations of Europe" but also a "struggle between political systems."[15] Germans, too, saw the conflict as one between the western democracies' idea of "civilization" and what they considered their own unique *Kultur*. They rejected "liberalism and individualism" in favor of the values of "duty, order, and justice," all of which required obedience to a powerful state.[16] They celebrated the voluntary subordination of the individual to the collective interests of the nation and denounced the selfishness and atomization of liberalism, the "all-powerful tyranny of individualism."[17] To the people of Britain, France, Holland, and Belgium, and to many in the United States, therefore, the war was not just a struggle for territory but for a way of life. Lippmann regarded German aggression as an attack "against the civilization of which we are a part" and on the "world system in which America lives."[18] That was what Wilson meant when he spoke of making the world "safe for democracy." It was not a utopian call for spreading democracy across the globe but a practical summons to defend the vulnerable democratic order of the "Atlantic community" that really was under siege.

Most Americans came to view the war as a struggle against authoritarianism and "militarism" on behalf of liberal civilization. And with such lofty goals, some degree of postwar disappointment and disillusionment was almost inevitable. The victorious Allies behaved as victorious powers always had, carving up territory, snapping up colonies, and punishing the defeated powers. It was not the "liberal peace" many Americans believed they had fought for, and so liberals on both sides of the Atlantic not only turned against the war but despaired of the possibility of a better world. The idea of progress was discredited. Millions of lives had been sacrificed, and for what? For a "botched civilization," as Ezra Pound memorably put it, for "an old bitch gone in the teeth."[19]

Although most Americans had enthusiastically supported entering the war, a majority decided afterward that it had been a terrible mistake and that tens of thousands of American soldiers had died for nothing. A search for someone to blame began, with many arguing that the public had been duped: by pro-British eastern newspapers and intellectuals, by financiers and munitions makers, by British agents inside the American government, and by a number of big lies, including the claim that Germany was primarily responsible for the war and that American vital interests would have been endangered by a German victory. "Wilson lied, people died" would have been a fair summary of the common view in many circles. Throughout the twenty years prior to World War II, the bitter controversy over America's intervention in World War I dominated all discussions of American foreign policy, much as the war in Iraq does today. Americans did not crawl into a hole after the war, but they rejected responsibility for the world's problems. Even the international agreements the United States signed, such as the Kellogg-Briand Pact "outlawing" war, were deliberately designed to avoid any American commitment to take action anywhere. Americans living on a vast, resource-rich continent separated from the other powers by two great oceans believed they had a choice to pull away from an increasingly violent and conflicted world.

The rest of the story is familiar enough. From 1933 to 1937, Hitler came to power in Germany, Japan invaded China, Mussolini's Italy invaded Ethiopia, Germany rearmed, the fascist powers intervened in Spain. Then in 1938 came the retreat of the democracies at Munich and in 1939 Germany's invasion of Poland. In the summer of 1940, France fell, British forces were driven from the continent, embarking the last forces from Dunkirk, and Hitler launched his attack on the British Isles.

Americans were reluctant to change course despite these unexpected developments. At first they clung to hopes that the situation would stabilize, that aggressors would see the folly of their ways or be beaten back, that the dictators would be toppled. As late as 1936, even hawkish internationalists like the former secretary of state and future secretary of war Henry Stimson refused to believe that Germany and Japan were "wholly lost to liberalism." Economic realities would force Hitler to limit his ambitions. And if that failed, Americans assumed that Britain and France would ultimately step up to the challenge. They did not believe those two great powers could be defeated by a Germany still recovering from the enforced disarmament of the Versailles Treaty. Looking back after the Second World War, Stimson still professed shock at the "extraordinary weakness and cowardice" of the European democracies, though without noting America's and his own failure to do anything while there still might have been a chance.[20]

It all happened so fast. Just four years after Stimson was still expressing "cautious optimism," Hitler had conquered the European continent and European democracy hung by a thread.[21] This shocking turn of events did not make Americans any more inclined to get involved. If anything, as the crises exploded, they became more determined to stay out. The costs of intervention went from unpalatable to intolerable. Experts predicted (correctly) that it would take millions of soldiers and cost unprecedented numbers of lives and resources to defeat a Germany that by the late spring of 1940 controlled everything from the Atlantic coast to the Black and

Baltic Seas. It would be almost as costly and dangerous to take on the increasingly powerful Japanese empire.

And even if the United States did intervene, would that solve the world's problems? Americans viewed Europe in those years the way they view the Arab world today, as hopelessly mired in ageless ethnic, national, and sectarian hatreds. It was the height of hubris, people like Senator Robert A. Taft argued, to believe the United States had the power or wisdom to bring peace and democracy to such a world. Europe would have to "work out its own salvation." Americans could not be running around the world like some "knight errant, protecting democracy and ideals of good faith, and tilting like Don Quixote against the windmills of fascism."[22] As Hans Morgenthau pointed out, Taft and others regarded themselves not as isolationists but as realists. They were dealing with the world as it was, not trying to transform it into what idealistic Americans wished it to be.[23] Members of the America First Committee—which included the future president of Yale Kingman Brewster, the writer Gore Vidal, the future Supreme Court justice Potter Stewart, and two future presidents of the United States, John F. Kennedy and Gerald Ford—rejected the idealism that had led their fathers' generation to war in 1917. As one historian of the movement notes, they regarded themselves as "smarter, more realistic."[24]

Internationalists argued that what was happening in Europe and Asia would ultimately come home to America's shores. Franklin Roosevelt warned that the world was descending into "a state of international anarchy and instability" from which there could be "no escape through mere isolation or neutrality." In June 1940, a week after the British evacuation from Dunkirk, he warned that a world where Nazi Germany dominated Europe and Imperial Japan dominated Asia would be for Americans a "helpless nightmare of a people without freedom—the nightmare of a people lodged in prison, hand-cuffed, hungry, and fed through the bars from day to day by the contemptuous, unpitying masters of other continents." In such a world, he warned, American democracy would not survive.[25] But anti-interventionists responded that it did not matter who controlled Europe. Americans could trade with Germany just as they did with England.[26]

And what if the United States did go to war, they asked, sent its armies across the ocean, landed its forces on a fortified continent against Hitler's battle-tested armies, and at some unimaginable cost managed to win? What then? Wouldn't American forces have to remain in Europe indefinitely to defend democracy and preserve the balance of power? Wouldn't the U.S. Navy have to "establish 'freedom of the seas' . . . on all the oceans"?[27] Would not policing the world after the war entail the endless expense of American "blood and treasure," not to mention a kind of "unadulterated imperialism" and "world-domination"?[28] Faced with these objections—which, it turned out, were not far off the mark in predicting America's postwar role—Roosevelt never fully succeeded in convincing Americans. He did manage to edge Americans toward providing greater and greater assistance to Britain in 1940 and 1941. But before Pearl Harbor, even with Hitler conquering Europe and Japan conquering Asia and the Pacific, the most gifted politician in American history never persuaded Americans that these were sufficient reasons to go to war.

.　　.　　.

Why does this history matter to us? The conventional wisdom these days is that we don't face anything like the kinds of threats that emerged in the 1930s. We comfort ourselves that Stalin and Hitler were one of a kind, that their like could never emerge in our world, and that even if they did we would respond appropriately, unlike those foolish "isolationists" of the 1930s. But the Americans of that earlier era also took comfort in such judgments. Few regarded Stalin as a monster in the 1920s or even in the 1930s, when little was known of the purges and the consequences of forced collectivization. Nor did most Americans regard European fascism in the 1920s and early 1930s as particularly dangerous or even evil. Mussolini enjoyed a certain vogue as the strong leader the Italian people needed, much as some American conservatives today admire Vladimir Putin for being a strong leader. Hitler struck some Americans as a dangerous extremist, but others saw him as a bulwark against communism, which they regarded as the more serious threat. Only very late did most come to regard Hitler as a menace, and even then few saw him as an existential threat to the United States and the democratic way of life.

The Americans who could not fully comprehend the dangers in their midst were not so different from us. They lived in a modern democratic capitalist society, informed by modern science and modern ways of understanding human behavior. They were kept aware of world events by an active press that reported on developments in Europe and Asia on a daily basis. The policy choices they made were not based on an unusual ignorance, therefore, or even on an unusual fecklessness. They had the same insight into the future that we have. They made their decisions based on normal hopes and fears, just as we do.

To them the risks and costs of action were obvious and immediate, while the costs of inaction were hazy and impossible to
know or prove in advance. Then as now, Americans worried
less about troubling geopolitical trends than about the state
of the economy and about being sucked into what they
regarded as misbegotten, costly, and ultimately fruitless foreign
wars. The only significant difference between us and them is
that we know what happened next. But had we been in their
shoes and known only what they knew, we would likely have
chosen the same course, catastrophic though it turned out
to be.

THE BIRTH OF THE NEW WORLD ORDER

World order is one of those things people don't think about
until it is gone. The experience of the 1930s and World War II
taught Americans that. They learned, and we have now forgotten, that when things start to go wrong, they can go very
wrong very quickly, that once a world order breaks down, the
worst qualities of humanity emerge from under the rocks and
run wild.

Americans before 1941 had barely realized that there was
a world order, much less that it was one from which they
benefited immensely. The nineteenth-century world in which
America had grown and prospered had rested on configura-
tions of power in the international system of which they had
been only dimly aware. One was the balance of power among
the European great powers that prevailed throughout much
of the nineteenth century following the Napoleonic Wars.
That uneasy balance had not prevented wars or turmoil—it

was not the "long peace" that some proclaim—but it had at least delayed the kind of world-shaking hegemonic conflicts among the great powers that had threatened American interests and security in the late eighteenth and early nineteenth centuries and would again in the two world wars of the twentieth.

The other key element of the old order had been Britain's domination of the world's oceanways. The liberal and commerce-minded British people had used their naval hegemony primarily to protect their global empire. But in keeping their own lines of trade and communication open, they had created and sustained a relatively open international economic order for everyone else, too. They provided the secure environment in which British and other bankers could extend finance to the United States and other developing nations and spread the benefits of innovations in communications, transportation, and production. The leading commercial nations on both sides of the Atlantic were thus pulled together into a mutually beneficial network which produced unprecedented levels of prosperity for the peoples of Western Europe and North America and made possible the liberal progress in the "Atlantic community" that so many celebrated at the dawn of the twentieth century. There was nothing very "liberal" about this order for those under British and other colonial rule, of course, and they reaped few if any of the benefits. But for Americans, the British order offered prosperity at almost no cost.

World orders do not last forever, however. They are the product of particular events and historical circumstances. Britain's near-monopoly of power on the oceans was the result of the defeat of France and Spain in the late eighteenth and early nineteenth centuries, while in Europe the great rival powers were precariously balanced against one another, which allowed the British to wield unusual influence even on the continent. In East Asia the old hegemon, China, was prostrate, and the future hegemon, Japan, was in self-imposed isolation. From the end of the Napoleonic Wars until the late nineteenth century, therefore, the British empire benefited from "a power-political vacuum."[29] This was a world in which a rapidly industrializing Britain could enjoy overwhelming economic and naval superiority and in which the United States could compete and eventually surpass the British hegemon itself.[30]

This exceptional situation could not last. By the turn of the century, Britain's primacy was being challenged from all directions, by the return of old rivals, France and Russia, and by new rising powers like Japan, the United States, and a unified Germany. The rise of Germany upset the balance of power on the continent, Russian power threatened the British position in India and the Near East, while the rise of Japan challenged British naval supremacy in East Asia and the Pacific. By the end of the nineteenth century, the foundations of European peace were gone, as was the Eurocentric world and the British-led liberal order. The world had undergone a radical redistribution of power of which World War I was a consequence, not the cause.

That global redistribution of power thrust the United States into an entirely new position in the international system. The order from which Americans had so greatly benefited could no longer be sustained by Britain alone. American interests remained the same, but to preserve those interests, to continue to prosper in relative security, would require the United States to take on a much more active role in the world and to wield the power that Britain no longer had. That, at least, was what people like Theodore Roosevelt, Woodrow Wilson, and other internationalists of the era believed at the beginning of the twentieth century, and World War I seemed to confirm it. In the fall of 1914, Roosevelt and others began to make the case that after the war was over the United States would have to become "one of the joint guarantors of world peace." It was not enough to seek only "our own defense," Roosevelt argued. Americans had to be ready to act in defense of others, too, whether "it be Germany or England, Belgium or Hungary, Russia or Japan." He saw America playing this role as part of a new consortium of great powers, an "international *posse comitatus*" to enforce some rules of behavior in an otherwise anarchic world—a "great World League for the Peace of Righteousness," he called it.[31] At about the same time Walter Lippmann concluded that the United States was going to have to take up the role that Britain could no longer play alone: to preserve the safety of the "Atlantic highway," to defend "the common interest" of the "Atlantic Community" and "the integrity of the Atlantic Powers." Americans were a member of "one great community," Lippmann argued, and they now had to be prepared to "defend the western world."[32] This was the principal purpose of Wilson's League of Nations, a new international institution through which American power could be exercised on behalf of a peaceful, liberal international order.

Neither Wilson nor most other internationalists sought such a role for the United States for its own sake. They believed the new geopolitics of the twentieth century left no choice. As the old liberal order sustained by Britain collapsed, the world would either descend into disorder or be dominated by nations hostile to American interests and principles. The only alternative was for the United States itself to play the central role in creating and defending a new liberal order, even if this meant shouldering new international responsibilities in perpetuity. This was not idealistic hubris. It was a practiced response to changing geopolitical circumstances.

A majority of Americans in 1919 had not relished such a role, and the Senate had rejected both the League of Nations and American participation in the Versailles settlement. After Pearl Harbor, however, the majority of Americans looked at the world differently. The Second World War not only ended the debate over whether the United States was physically secure from attack, but it convinced most Americans that Wilson and the two Roosevelts had been right: Americans and their way of life could not be safe in a world where Europe and Asia were dominated by hostile autocratic powers.[33]

Most Americans now agreed that the new configuration of power in the world and the new technologies of warfare, communications, and economics required a new global strategy. It was no longer sufficient for the United States to sit "in the parlor with a loaded shotgun, waiting," as Dean Acheson put it. Americans lived "right smack in the middle" of an increasingly interconnected world and would invariably be dragged into its conflicts, whether they wished to be or not.[34] To safeguard its interests and its way of life, therefore, the United States would have to extend its security frontier far from its shores and into those regions of the world where the threats were likely to emerge. American strategy had to become proactive rather than passive, aimed at shaping the international environment, not just reacting to it.

Beginning as early as 1943 military planners drew up proposals for a postwar network of bases in the Pacific and the Atlantic from which any potential aggressor could be attacked and defeated at the source.[35] As Roosevelt put it that year, if the United States did not "pull the fangs of the predatory animals of this world," they would "multiply and grow in strength" and would "be at our throats again once more in a short generation."[36]

The result was not only a new military strategy but the establishment of a new world order designed to prevent a return to the international condition that had produced two world wars and threatened America's democratic capitalist system. America's new approach to the world rested on the belief that it was not enough to defend the nation's physical security or its domestic economy, or even its access to raw materials and overseas markets. To protect the "American experiment of life," Acheson argued, required creating "an environment of freedom" in the world beyond America's shores.[37] This was not just a geographical space but also a political, economic, and ideological space, Lippmann's "Atlantic Community," with democratic governments on both shores united by common strategic objectives and a common commitment to an open economic system and a liberal political order.

The economic aspect of the order was essential. Acheson and others believed the "derangement of the international economy" in the 1920s and 1930s had been a major cause of global conflict. Germany and Japan had worked to establish self-contained economic zones to make themselves independent of commercial and financial dealings with the Western powers and to enhance their hegemony over their neighbors.

The United States and the Western democracies had played their part by turning increasingly to protectionism in the 1920s. The resulting economic nationalism and competing economic blocs had compounded geopolitical competition, reduced cooperation, and lowered standards of living, giving rise to nationalist populism and radicalism. If this pattern persisted after the war, Acheson warned in early 1945, the United States would have to adopt a managed, autarkic economy of its own, which "would completely change our Constitution, our relations to property, human liberty, our very conception of law." To prevent "the division of the world into warring economic blocs" and to ensure the survival of the "American experiment," as well as global markets for American goods, required an open international economy. "To construct a peace," Acheson argued in the final months of the war, there had to be "an economic peace as well as a political and military peace."[38]

To create and sustain an "environment of freedom" naturally required support for democracy as well—not everywhere, but in critical parts of the world. The "Atlantic Community" had to be comprised of democracies, which meant not only protecting existing democratic governments in Britain and France but also in Italy and other parts of Western and Central Europe where traditions of democracy were either weak or nonexistent. It also meant imposing democratic government on Germany and Japan after the war. Americans since the days of the founders had always believed that autocratic governments were more prone to war than democracies. Acheson believed the Imperial Japanese regime had helped create a "will to war" among the people, and few doubted that this had been true of Nazi Germany.[39]

The Americans who established the contours of this new grand strategy believed they were pursuing America's national interests, and they were. But their approach transcended traditional notions of national interest. Throughout history and for the vast majority of states, the national interest had been defined in a limited way, as defense of the state's immediate physical and economic security. Great powers construed their interests more broadly than weaker powers, to include spheres of influence or regional economic hegemony, but the purposes were roughly the same. America's new strategy went well beyond traditional national interests. It entailed the creation and defense of a liberal international order. It meant accepting "international responsibility" for protecting the interests not only of the United States but of others who shared Americans' worldview. Catastrophe had come in the 1930s, people like Harry Truman believed, because Americans had not accepted "our responsibility as a world power."[40]

Critics at the time and later complained that the idea of assuming international responsibility was antithetical to American interests.[41] And it was true that few nations in history had ever regarded it as their responsibility to uphold a political, economic, and strategic order, much less in regions of the world that were thousands of miles from their borders. Normal nations did not have "international responsibilities." For most of its history the United States had been normal in that sense. This new grand strategy made the United States exceptional.

It was exceptional less because the American people were exceptional than because America's position in the twentieth-century world had become exceptional. A combination of geography, natural resources, and a liberal capitalist economic system adept at producing wealth gave Americans a unique and unprecedented capacity to influence global affairs. Because it was effectively an island power, surrounded on two sides by water and on the other two sides by weaker nations, the United States faced no immediate threats to its security. Thousands of miles separated it from the world's other great powers, which, by contrast, were bunched together and existed in a perpetual state of insecurity and anxiety about one another. Because it was so secure, the United States had been able to grow rich without fear of plunder by its neighbors, and because it grew rich, it also had the capacity to grow strong militarily, if and when it chose.

These unique circumstances had allowed Americans to remain aloof from the world when that seemed safe and possible, but when that ceased to be a safe course, as the two world wars demonstrated, the same circumstances also allowed them to shape the world in an unprecedented manner. Because of its geographical position, the United States had the unique ability to deploy the bulk of its military forces thousands of miles away for long stretches of time. All the other great powers had to keep their forces close to home lest they leave themselves vulnerable to their neighbors. This disparity meant that the other great powers engaged in their regional competitions with one another could look to the United States for assistance, as France and Britain did in 1914 and 1939, as China did in its struggle with Japan in the 1930s and 1940s, and as Japan, Korea, and other Asian powers do today in response to a rising China, and as Eastern Europe does in response to an aggressive Russia. The United States could play the role of deus ex machina in Asia and Europe, and in the Middle East, simultaneously, without inviting an invasion of its homeland. No other nation in history had ever played this role because no other nation could have. The United States itself could not have done it before the twentieth century. Americans had rejected this role in 1919 and for the two decades that followed. Now, as a result of the rude awakening of Pearl Harbor and their involvement in the Second World War, they fundamentally accepted it.

There was nothing inevitable about the choice they made after 1945, however. Not only had Americans made a different choice in 1919, but so had other great powers in comparable situations. Even Great Britain at the height of its power had not taken on such a responsibility where it mattered most, on the European continent. Although the British had, in theory, played a balancing role in Europe in the eighteenth and nineteenth centuries, they had never really taken responsibility for preserving peace on the continent, even though it was but twenty miles from its shores, not three thousand. The British had not kept their forces in Europe after the defeat of Napoleon; they had not deterred the rise of German hegemony on the continent following the defeat of France in 1871; they had not made a commitment to defend France before 1914; and they had not guaranteed European security after the First World War. Given how much more secure Americans were behind the two oceans than Britain was behind the Channel, their eventual willingness to shoulder responsibility for preserving the general peace in both Europe and Asia was all the more extraordinary.

They made this choice, moreover, before the onset of the Cold War. This would be forgotten almost immediately and remain forgotten for the next seven decades, but most Americans accepted this new internationalist approach to the world even before they thought the Soviet Union would be an adversary. They agreed to found and participate in the new United Nations organization, a modified form of the League they had rejected in 1919, at a time when most expected the United States and the Soviet Union under Stalin to continue cooperating. "We are going to get along very well with him and the Russian people," Roosevelt said at the end of 1943, "very well indeed."[42] Even in 1945 Acheson and others inside and outside government assumed the postwar world would be kept at peace by the three great powers that had carried the brunt of the war against Germany and Japan—the United States, Britain, and the Soviet Union.

The new strategy was not directed toward any particular new threat or against any particular country.[43] Its chief purpose was to prevent a return to the economic, political, and strategic circumstances that had given rise to the last war. It was a response to the geopolitical realities of the twentieth century.

It was also a response to the human condition, to the enduring realities of human nature and the behavior of nations. The architects of the new order were in many ways pessimists when it came to their assessment of humanity and the nature of international relations. While many Americans put their faith in the new United Nations and looked forward to a system of laws and institutions that would eventually replace force in the conduct of international affairs, people like Roosevelt, Truman, Acheson, George C. Marshall, and George F. Kennan generally did not. The experience of the previous four decades had left them with few illusions. Americans,

Roosevelt insisted, must no longer cling to "pious hopes that aggressor and warlike nations would learn and understand" the virtues of peace, as the proponents of such agreements as the Kellogg-Briand Pact "outlawing war" had hoped they would.[44] The world was an international jungle, Acheson argued, with no "rules, no umpire, no prizes for good boys." In such a world, weakness and indecision were "fatal," the "judgment of nature upon error" was death. Nor would there be any escape from this reality, ever: no self-sustaining international balance of power to preserve peace, no self-regulating legal order, no end to international struggle and competition. Such security as was possible, both physical security and the security of liberal ideals, could be preserved only by meeting power with greater power. In the world as it was configured, the only guarantee of peace, Acheson insisted, was "the continued moral, military and economic power of the United States." As he would later put it, the United States was "the locomotive at the head of mankind."[45]

The architects of the postwar order were realists in this sense, therefore, but it was a realism in the service of liberalism, of ideals and principles that they believed were universal and irrefutable. They hoped that if the base and destructive elements of human nature could be contained and suppressed, and the better elements protected and nurtured, then the possibilities for human progress—moral, political, and material—could be unleashed. In this respect they were much like the founders of the republic. Alexander Hamilton and James Madison were true believers in the Enlightenment principles proclaimed in Jefferson's Declaration of Independence. "The sacred rights of mankind," Hamilton proclaimed, were "written, as with a sunbeam, in the whole volume of human nature by the hand of the divinity itself."[46] But the system of government they tried to erect did not depend on the triumph of the better angels of human nature. The competition for power and advantage among different groups with different interests was "sown in the nature of man," Madison argued.[47] Hence the need for a system of checks and balances that would set ambition against ambition and contain humanity's destructive impulses. If such a well-ordered polity could be established, then progress would be possible, including the fulfillment of the Declaration's promise of universal rights.

The founders of the postwar order believed in those universalist principles, and they further had no doubt about the superiority of democratic capitalism over socialism or fascism or any other alternative system of political economy. But after witnessing the rise of Hitler, Stalin, and Mussolini and the near collapse of both democracy and capitalism in the 1930s, they did not believe that liberal ideals would triumph simply because they were right and true. They did not share the optimism of some of the internationalist idealists of their day, and of ours, who believed that commerce and democracy alone, or laws and treaties outlawing war, or institutions like the U.N. could be relied on to shape the behavior of peoples and nations. They believed that peace, prosperity, and progress depended on the exercise of power, and specifically American power.

Yet they also differed from the realists of the 1930s, and of our own time. They did believe progress was possible, and they rejected the fatalism that served as an excuse for inaction in the face of rising fascist powers. They believed it had been a mistake to reject the League of Nations and the Versailles

Treaty, however flawed they may have been. Even an imperfect liberal order was preferable to no order at all or to one dominated by liberalism's opponents.[48] As Roosevelt said before his death in 1945, Americans needed to have "the courage to fulfill our responsibilities in an admittedly imperfect world."[49] Liberal progress was possible, but it required the creation and preservation of a favorable international order, backed by power, in which the better elements of human nature could be nurtured and protected and allowed to flourish.

LIFE INSIDE THE LIBERAL ORDER

The price that would have to be paid to create and sustain this new order turned out to be higher than its founders had imagined, and certainly higher than the American public believed when it signed up for these new international responsibilities. Many Americans did imagine that the mere founding of the United Nations represented the dawn of a new era of peace. They assumed that the victorious powers would cooperate to sustain the new order. And even Roosevelt believed that the role of the United States, though central, would consist chiefly of leading the other nations in a cooperative effort, as he had done during the war. America's military contribution to keeping the peace, though substantial, would be largely a matter of deploying naval and air power in the key theaters in support of the other great powers—Britain, Russia, and China. When the war ended, Truman believed, along with the great majority of Americans, that American soldiers could be brought home and the massive expenditures on defense could be cut dramatically.

Not even the keenest observers of the international scene had quite anticipated the far more difficult postwar realities. They had not planned on Britain's weakness or comprehended that it would never fully recover from the geopolitical transformations of the late nineteenth century, much less from the physical and psychological trauma of the two world wars.[50] Western Europe was in much worse shape than anyone had imagined. Economies were devastated, as were the populations that would have to revive them. China, meanwhile, was in the throes of civil war and revolution, and could not possibly play a stabilizing role in East Asia. Instead of relying on these other "policemen" to sustain the new international order, therefore, Americans suddenly found themselves serving as the central organizer and administrator, the principal provider of military power, and for a time the sole funder of the new order.

It is not at all clear that they would have accepted this role, and persisted in it for four-plus decades, had it not been for the most significant unanticipated development of all: the emergence of the Soviet Union as an ideological and geopolitical adversary rather than the partner Roosevelt had expected. The Cold War confrontation meant that the task of creating and sustaining a new liberal world order was going to be more difficult and demanding.

The onset of the Cold War, however, did not change the grand strategy on which Americans had already embarked. The deployment of American troops in both Europe and Asia, the expenditure of billions of dollars to help foreign economies get back on their feet, and the extensive global engagement of the United States would have been necessary to sustain the new liberal world order even if there had never been a Cold War.

In Europe this meant accepting the responsibility Americans had rejected in 1919. No "environment of freedom" could be created and sustained if the major nations on the other shore of the Atlantic were not democratic. But Americans and Europeans feared that Western Europe would not remain democratic if its economy did not recover from the devastation of the war. And the Western European economy could not recover unless the German economy was allowed to recover. This was a problem. Britain and France and Germany's other neighbors feared that a revived German economy would only lead to revived German power and ambition. In Europe at mid-century, even the new threat posed by the Soviet Union was not as worrying as the threat of a powerful, united, militaristic Germany. To shore up a prosperous and democratic Western Europe, therefore, required guaranteeing those nations' security against Germany—exactly what the United States had refused to do after 1918. After 1945, it also required protecting Western Europe, including the new West Germany, against Soviet power and influence. It was the European powers that first broached the idea of a defense alliance with the United States, and Marshall, Acheson, and most other policymakers quickly decided that this was indeed the only solution both to the old German problem and to the new Soviet problem. The United States thus helped revive Western European economies with the Marshall Plan, but it also established the NATO alliance to preserve a lasting peace in Europe. As Marshall observed, the American military occupation of Europe would have to be of "indefinite duration" in order to provide the "protracted security guarantees" necessary to establish "a firm community of interests."[51]

The story in Asia was much the same. Americans' initial

aim was simply to destroy Japanese military power as well
as the autocratic system and way of life that Americans
believed had produced Japanese militarism. But after the
Chinese Revolution in 1949 and the North Korean invasion of the South in 1950, American policymakers quickly
came to see a reformed, stable, and prosperous Japan as the
key to broader Asian stability. Just as with Germany, however, Japan's economic revival was a frightening prospect to
its wartime victims, and they insisted on a reliable American
guarantee against the return of Japanese power and ambition. The United States signed security treaties with Australia,
New Zealand, and the Philippines in 1951, at their request,
promising to defend them against either communist or Japanese aggression. The security treaty signed with Japan in 1951
enshrined a continued U.S. military presence and effectively
subordinated the Japanese military (such as it was) to American control. For the United States, the treaties were primarily about containing communism, but for the powers in the
region, they were mostly about containing Japan.[52]

The historic consequences of these decisions to keep American troops in Europe and Asia were barely comprehended at
the time and have been largely overlooked ever since. Americans then and later were so focused on the Cold War that they
did not see how their actions produced a revolution in the
international system and set history off on a different trajectory. America's postwar policies, beginning before the onset
of the Cold War but deepening and intensifying after 1946,
created new geopolitical realities and new patterns of international behavior. The spiral of conflict that had begun with

the rise of Germany and Japan and the collapse of the British world order at the end of the nineteenth century was halted. The radical reorientation of the two defeated powers, and the introduction of American power into Europe and East Asia on a permanent basis, put an end to the cycles of conflict that twice in three decades had sucked almost the entire world into the maelstrom. In retrospect, the most significant postwar revolution in international affairs was not the new Cold War confrontation between the United States and the Soviet Union but the gradual transformation of Germany and Japan from the ambitious, autocratic, military powerhouses they had been to the pacific, democratic, economic powerhouses they eventually became.

This transformation was not initially the result of a natural evolution in either country. It was the consequence both of military defeat and of postwar American and Allied policies. The devastation suffered by the German and Japanese people went far to discredit the regimes that had brought it upon them. Yet it is doubtful that democracy would have come naturally to Germany and Japan had it not been for the occupation and enduring presence of American troops. Democratic traditions in both countries were weak and relatively new. Such Japanese democracy as had emerged in the 1920s had been easily swept aside by militarist, authoritarian forces. In Germany, even during the Weimar period, many Germans felt no deep attachment to the republic, and it had been easily dismantled after 1930, even before Hitler's accession to power in 1933. Nor had there been much resistance to Nazi rule before the last months of the war. After the war, there were many committed democrats in Germany and Japan, but there were also many who were not committed. The denazification program in Germany and the purge of militarists and ultra-nationalists in Japan, though flawed and incomplete, sent a powerful message to both societies. Whether or not former Nazis and pro-Nazis became democrats, the American occupation left them no alternative but to behave like democrats, and that turned out to be good enough.[53] In West Germany by the 1960s, the great majority of citizens were unquestionably democrats in spirit as well as in form, and today are arguably among the most liberal people in the world. (By way of comparison, in East Germany, under Soviet occupation, the Nazi dictatorship simply became an even more totalitarian communist dictatorship.)

The shift in Germany's and Japan's geopolitical trajectories, meanwhile, changed the global strategic environment in ways that were ultimately more significant and more lasting than the rise and fall of the Soviet Union. Article 9 of the new, American-drafted Japanese constitution stated in the first paragraph that Japan "forever renounce[d] war as a sovereign right of the nation and the threat or use of force as a means of settling international disputes."[54] Germany under American and Allied occupation in the West, and under Soviet occupation in the East, also gave up its independence as a player on the international scene. This effectively precluded the option of returning to past patterns of behavior. Whether these transformations would have occurred had the United States not used its power to impose "demilitarization and democratization" in both countries is unlikely. Had Americans returned home after the war, there is no telling what path those two countries might have taken.

The effect on the two regions in which these powers had arisen was revolutionary. Denying a geopolitical and military path to Germany and Japan provided a level of security to their neighbors that they had not known for decades. With the United States also providing the bulk of the deterrent against the Soviets, the nations of Europe and the East were suddenly liberated to focus their energies and resources on domestic and economic matters rather than on the strategic concerns that had consumed them in the first half of the twentieth century.

Germany and Japan were also liberated. With geopolitical ambitions and the military route to power and influence foreclosed, they, too, could channel all their energies and ambitions into the achievement of economic success and domestic welfare. This was a conscious American objective. As then Secretary of State James Byrnes put it in 1946, "freedom from militarism" gave the German people the chance "to apply their great energies and abilities to the works of peace."[55] In Japan, economic expertise replaced military expertise as the most valued skill. The Ministry of Trade and Industry became more important than the Ministry of Foreign Affairs. Japanese corporations that had produced the tanks, trucks, and warships that allowed Japan to conquer Asia converted to the production of automobiles, commercial vessels, and other civilian manufactured goods that formed the basis of the Japanese economic "miracle." The loss of empire forced corporate leaders to plan new market strategies that proved remarkably successful. What the historian John Dower has written of Japan—that it "benefited from losing"—could be said of both defeated powers. But they were not the only ones who benefited. American policy aimed to transform the two into what Acheson called the "workshops" of Europe and Asia. Their growing economies became engines for broader

European, Asian, and ultimately global economic growth in what would become the most prosperous period in the history of humankind.[56] From having been the great disrupters of peace and order, Germany and Japan became champions of a new political and economic order of which they were among the greatest beneficiaries.

The democratization, pacification, and economic resuscitation of Germany and Japan, along with the introduction of American power into the previously conflicted regions of Europe and East Asia, transformed not only the global power structure but also the very dynamics of international relations. Within the confines of the new order, normal geopolitical competition all but ceased. The nations of Western Europe and East Asia did not engage in arms races; they did not form strategic alliances against one another; they did not claim strategic or economic spheres of influence; there were no "security dilemmas" driven by mutual apprehension and insecurity; no balance of power was required to preserve the peace among them.

Just as importantly, within this burgeoning liberal order, the normal link between economics and geopolitics was severed. Throughout history, fluctuations in economic power among the great states, nations, and empires had always produced upheaval and war. As nations grew richer relative to others, or as they grew more technologically advanced, these gains translated into increased military power and global influence. "Rich nation, strong army" was the Japanese motto as it began to reform and modernize in the late nineteenth century, and the phrase was borrowed from a Chinese saying going back centuries. Whatever balance of power that previously existed was upset, and the result was frequently a war that created a new balance reflecting the new hierarchy of power, which in turn reflected the new economic and technological hierarchy.[57] In the new liberal order, which at first included chiefly the United States, Western Europe, and Japan, nations competed economically and tried to out-manufacture, out-innovate, and out-sell each other. But that economic competition did not translate into military or geopolitical competition. In a normal world, the Japanese and German economic miracles would have led one or both to challenge the order and its hierarchy. In the new liberal order they did not.

This was not just because Germany, Japan, and other European and Asian powers were allied to the United States against the Soviet Union and China, nor was it just because the United States was more powerful and kept the other powers in check. After all, by the 1970s, the combined economies of the Western European powers and Japan equaled or exceeded that of the United States. Historically, alliances rarely survive such large shifts in economic power. Had the other major powers in the liberal order chosen to translate their new economic power into military power, they could have posed a formidable resistance to American hegemony—especially if they were willing to work with the Soviet Union. That they did not spoke to the unique attributes of the liberal order, and also of American behavior within it.

America's permanent strategic engagement, the fact that it was "onshore" with its troops based in Europe and Asia, as opposed to being the "offshore balancer" that Britain had tried unsuccessfully to be in the nineteenth and twentieth centuries, was a critical factor. Among the reasons that growing wealth had always led to growing military power and eventually to geopolitical conflict was that nations could rely only on themselves for their security. Since economic competition and the fluctuations of economic power were constant, and since prior to 1945 most great powers translated their economic power into military power, nations with growing economies invariably had to take advantage of the opportunity to get ahead of their potential adversaries. In the new circumstances established by the United States after the war, however, those nations within the American security order did not have to worry about keeping up with their neighbors militarily. The American alliance system and military deployments protected them from one another, as well as from threats outside the order. Had either Germany or Japan sought to translate economic power into military power, they would have immediately aroused fears among their neighbors. In the past, those neighbors would have had no recourse except to arm themselves and enter into an arms race—as they had in the decades leading up to the First World War. In the new order, however, they could look to the United States to bring its power to bear on their behalf, if necessary. But it never was necessary. The American role in the world reassured weaker powers and deterred rising economic powerhouses from contemplating a challenge to the system. As a result, all could take part in the global economic competition, alternately pulling ahead and falling behind, without fear of the strategic consequences.

Within the liberal order, there were also no geopolitical and strategic spheres of interest. In the past, struggles over overlapping spheres of interest had often been the source of great-power conflicts. The First World War in Europe and the

Second World War in Europe and Asia were initially fought over such contested regions as the Balkans, Poland, the provinces of Alsace and Lorraine, and Czechoslovakia. In East Asia it was Japan's claim to a sphere of interest on the Asian mainland, first in Korea and then in China beginning with the northern province of Manchuria—a claim that was not so unreasonable given the spheres already claimed by the European powers in China and Southeast Asia.

Looking back from the perspective of 1945, however, international acquiescence to Germany's and Japan's demands, legitimate or not, looked like a terrible mistake, the beginning of a long string of concessions that ended in the very war that appeasement of those demands was supposed to prevent. The postwar settlement did not allow Germany and Japan any spheres of interest, therefore, just as it did not allow them geopolitical ambitions. The whole tenor of the new liberal order ran against spheres of influence, even for the victorious powers. The exception was the peculiar role of the United States, which as guarantor of the order essentially claimed the whole world as its sphere of interest, and especially once the Cold War emerged. But other historic spheres of interest eroded under the combined pressure of liberal norms and the geopolitical dynamics, even if that was not the stated intent of the peace settlement. As one State Department memorandum put it in July 1945, a return to spheres of interest would be a return to "power politics pure and simple." America's objective should be "to remove the causes which make nations feel that such spheres are necessary to build their security."[58]

This included even the centuries-old British and French empires. The worldwide anticolonial struggle waged by peoples seeking independence from colonial rule was one of the great transformative forces of the twentieth century. But it was not inevitable that those liberation movements should have succeeded in wresting their independence when they did. Had the world continued as before, with the multipolar competition among the great powers, both Britain and France would likely have clung more tenaciously to their empires, as they had in the past when faced with independence movements. In the nineteenth and early twentieth centuries, they had regarded their colonies as vital strategic assets—in Britain's case as a source of economic power and international basing for its global fleet; for France as a means of augmenting a population that was dangerously declining in comparison with Germany's. In the new configuration of power after World War II, however, with British and French security guaranteed by the United States, with the seas kept open by the American navy, with the two former great powers too weak to defend their empires and the Americans eventually uninterested in doing it for them, both the sustainability and the strategic value of the colonies disappeared. It is doubtful that new liberal anticolonial "norms" would alone have changed European minds, since colonial rule was not anathema to all liberal Britons before, during, or even after the war.[59] It was the new world order that helped kill those empires off. Britain and France gave up their global spheres of interest, and Germany and Japan lost theirs, and none of these powers sought to regain what they had lost. It was a remarkable and historically unprecedented shift in the approaches of these once-dominant world powers.

The success of the order, however, also depended on the United States abiding by some basic rules. Chief among these was that it not exploit the system it dominated to gain lasting economic advantages at the expense of the other powers in the order. Put simply, it could not use its military dominance to win the economic competition against fellow members of the order, nor could it treat the economic competition as a zero-sum game and insist on always winning. This did not mean it could not compete. Nor did it preclude certain measures of protectionism—which almost all nations practiced even in a "free trade" regime—or currency devaluations and other measures that might provide advantages. The United States certainly benefited from being the dominant player in the international economy as well as the dominant player militarily. But a key element holding the order together was the perception by the other powers that they had a reasonably fair chance to succeed economically and sometimes even to surpass the United States—as Japan, Germany, and other nations did at various times. The determined postwar American effort to reconstruct the German, Western European, and Japanese economies produced a vigorous "intercapitalist competition" which would eventually force American companies to compete even harder to maintain profitability.[60] From 1950 to 1970, industrial production in Western Europe expanded at an average annual rate of 7.1 percent. Annual GDP rose by 5.5 percent; per capita GDP by 4.4 percent. These growth rates "exceeded anything previously known in Europe." These growing economies would, together with the United States, make the liberal world order a formidable and even dominant force in the global economy. It also made them capable of going toe-to-toe with the United States in some major facets of the global economic competition.[61] By the mid-1960s, both Germany and Japan had pulled ahead of the United

States in a number of key industries, from automobiles to steel production to consumer electronics.[62]

In the 1980s per capita income in East Asia, not including Japan, increased by almost 40 percent compared to that of the other major powers of the liberal order.[63] After 1950, the Korean War prompted the United States to establish a regional trade and assistance regime favorable to Japan, which set in train not only the Japanese "miracle" but the success of the Asian "tigers" of South Korea, Taiwan, Singapore, and Hong Kong in the 1970s and 1980s, and of China and Vietnam thereafter.[64] The result was that over the course of the Cold War the United States saw its share of global GDP fall from over 50 percent to under 25 percent even as America's GDP grew and Americans generally prospered. This was the direct consequence of American policies, and it was essential to the health of the liberal order. Had the order systematically served American interests at the expense of the other members, it's not clear it could have survived. The other nations in the system might have reacted more as international relations theory predicted, joining together to balance against the dominant power and seeking to undermine its hegemony. For the liberal order to succeed, others had to want to be part of it, and that meant providing a relatively fair field of competition. The United States could not be in the game to win every point. It had to be willing to cooperate in ways that might sometimes offer greater benefits to others. In economic matters, at least, it was not simply "America First." As Roosevelt put it at the opening of the Bretton Woods Conference that established the institutions and the terms of the new open economic order, "the economic health of every country is a proper concern to all its neighbors, near and far."[65]

This was the difference between taking on "international

responsibility" for a liberal order and pursuing national interests in a normal, traditional manner. If America's interest was in the preservation of a liberal order, as Americans believed it was after the Second World War, then other liberal powers had to be relatively content with the operation of the order. This meant taking part in institutions, such as the United Nations, which other nations might value more than American policymakers did. Embedding the United States within such institutions, including an international trade regime, was a way of softening the edges of America's preponderant power within the system. It was a nod to a more democratic system for setting international policies, even if the United States held the upper hand on many questions. As the historian John Lewis Gaddis has noted, American political leaders and policymakers, having grown up in a democratic system, had the "habits of democracy" and were used to managing partnerships through "persuasion, negotiation, and compromise." The United States often got its way, but not always, and many American initiatives in the immediate postwar years originated with their European allies.[66] Such participation by the United States helped knit the members of the liberal order into what they could regard as a common international community. This proved to be a key advantage in the Cold War confrontation. A major weakness of the Soviet empire was that important members of the Warsaw Pact were not content with the Soviet order, and as soon as they had a chance to defect, they took it.

It was not that America's allies were completely content within the order either, of course. America's willingness to compete on a relatively equal plane in economic matters did not extend to all areas, and it particularly did not apply to strategic issues. American administrations from Truman and Dwight Eisenhower to Jimmy Carter and Ronald Reagan insisted on making the critical decisions with regard to the Cold War confrontation, for instance, and also in dealing with what the United States regarded as recalcitrant nations within the order. It discouraged and in some cases prohibited independent European efforts to seek a relaxation of tensions with the Soviet Union. It carried out military interventions and covert operations to thwart perceived communist advances, usually without seeking the acquiescence of other members of the order and sometimes over the objections of many. The multilateralism it practiced on economic matters it rarely practiced on matters of security.[67]

People today like to look back nostalgically at the "rules-based" order supposedly established by the United States after World War II. But on strategic issues, the order was not always "rules-based" for America. When it deemed it necessary, rightly or wrongly, the United States violated the rules, including those it claimed to uphold, whether conducting military interventions without U.N. authorization, as it did several times during the Cold War, or engaging in covert activities that had no international sanction.

Critics at home and abroad condemned this American hypocrisy and the ways the order fell short of liberal ideals. Many favored a postwar order that was more genuinely democratic and gave all members an equal say on all international matters. Some believed international justice required a balance of power, and that American hegemony was both unjust and unsustainable. They worried that Americans would be corrupted by their excessive power. Throughout the Cold

War, and after, there were questions about the legitimacy of an order that claimed to be rules-based but was often shaped by the American hegemon's perception of its own interests. During the Vietnam War, millions of Europeans went into the streets to condemn American policy; in the Reagan years, millions more protested the deployment of American intermediate range nuclear missiles in Europe. In the 1960s France under de Gaulle pulled out of NATO and West Germany's chancellor Willy Brandt pursued an *Ostpolitik* of rapprochement with East Germany and the Soviet Union that defied American wishes. Some in Western Europe pressed for a more neutral posture in order to escape American strategic hegemony and avoid what they feared was a coming clash between the two superpowers, with Europe as the battleground. These days many talk about returning to an inter-Allied harmony that never quite existed as they imagine it.

Despite all this, however, despite the shortcomings of the order and of America's often high-handed behavior, none of the major players within the liberal order sought to leave it or challenge it. France left the NATO military structure but did not cease cooperating with the United States and the other NATO allies and did not in any sense become neutral. Germany, even during the period of *Ostpolitik*, never gave up its strong ties to the alliance and to the United States. In the 1980s the controversial decision to deploy American missiles in Europe, however much opposed by many Europeans, was driven at least as much by the leaders of Britain, France, and Germany as by the United States.

Partly the decision to stay was pragmatic. To challenge the order would have required massive rearmament, a diversion of resources from civilian to military production, and a shift in national priorities from social welfare to defense, none of which the other major powers were interested in undertaking. But it was more than that. In the decades before the First World War and during the interwar years, Britain, France, and Japan had consistently maintained large militaries and devoted sizable percentages of their national wealth to military spending. After the war, they could easily have returned to past patterns without either bankrupting themselves or dismantling their social welfare systems.[68] Had the United States withdrawn behind the oceans after the war, they would surely have done so. Yet it was precisely their past history that Europeans after the Second World War sought to escape. Having fought two world wars in less than four decades and having twice brought European civilization to the brink of annihilation, at the expense of hundreds of millions of lives and incalculable material costs, they wanted a new era of peace and cooperation. The new American order gave them the chance.

To criticize this as free-riding is to miss the profound and historically transformative choice they were making. The American security guarantee provided the opportunity to end the cycle of multipolar military competition that had culminated in two world wars. For most Europeans, even a flawed American world order was preferable to that. If they often did not acknowledge this, even to themselves, they proved it every day with their declining defense budgets and their continued voluntary participation in the American security order. It was not only that they preferred that order to the Soviet order. They could have carved out their own order between the two, as some Europeans would indeed have preferred. European neutralism was an option if Western Europeans had genuinely wanted it and been willing to arm themselves sufficiently to pursue it. That they did not pursue this third way but remained firmly in the American camp, both during and after the Cold War, was a tacit acknowledgment by Europeans, freshly emerged from their latest catastrophic war, that they could not erect a stable, peaceful, liberal order on their own. As the historian Odd Arne Westad observes, Europeans were "convinced that the U.S. military presence within their own borders helped keep the peace and develop democracies."[69]

None of this would have been possible, however, if Europeans had not fundamentally trusted the Americans. They did not fear American aggression against them, despite America's overwhelming military power, nor did they fear that the United States would attempt to divide and rule, as imperial powers of the past had always done. As Jean Monnet commented, it was "the first time in history that a great power, instead of basing its policy on ruling by dividing, ha[d] consistently and resolutely backed the creation of a large Community uniting peoples previously apart."[70] This was something unique. Even when Britain and France had been allies and fought together twice against Germany, they never stopped regarding each other as imperial competitors and as possible military threats. No such concerns were directed at the United States. Europeans also trusted America not to exploit its superior power at their expense. Although Americans were selfish, like any people, the Europeans recognized that American presidents, at least, were acting on a more complex and expansive definition of self-interest. The United States was invested in preserving an order that, to work, had to enjoy some degree of voluntary acceptance by its members—not a competition of all against all but a community of like-minded nations acting together to preserve a system from which all could benefit. Flawed as this system might be—flawed as the Americans were—in the real world this was as good as it was likely to get. Or at least that was the general view during the Cold War. The order held together because the other members regarded American hegemony, by any realistic standards, as relatively benign, and superior to the alternatives.

The liberal order also held together because it was liberal. Although Europeans generally regarded the American system as a more brutal, atomizing form of capitalism, and Americans generally regarded the European social welfare state as excessively impinging on the free market and individual choice, these were disagreements within a common liberal home. Their collective commitment to democratic capitalism—no Western European nation ever became "socialist"—and their dedication to the rights of the individual against the state were a powerful bond that made it easier for both sides to understand and trust one another. They shared the same broad hopes and expectations for human progress and pursued a similar journey, albeit at varying paces. States and societies within the liberal order became more humane in the treatment of citizens and even of criminals, increasingly respectful of free speech, a free press, and the right to protest and dissent. The poor were better cared for. Rights were continually expanded to hitherto unprotected minorities. Racialism and tribalism were dampened in favor of a growing cosmopolitanism. Extreme forms of nationalism diminished. The liberal world was far from perfect—injustice and inequity persisted, along with killing, bigotry, and brutality, in the United States and elsewhere. It was still the City of Man and not the City of God—which was enough for critics of liberalism on left and right to declare it a failure. But compared to the previous five thousand years, it was a revolutionary transformation of human existence.

There was a self-reinforcing quality to the progress that occurred within the order. As liberal norms evolved, liberal nations came under pressure to live up to them, including the United States. It was no accident that the greatest advances in American civil rights occurred in the decades after World War II. Americans had fought a war against racism, but racism persisted in America. It received widespread coverage in the world press and criticism from America's democratic allies. The Cold War competition also played a big part, as the Soviet Union deployed American racism as a weapon in its campaigns against American "imperialism," especially in Africa and other predominantly nonwhite regions of the world. The hard work, courage, and sacrifice of African Americans and civil rights leaders were buttressed by the attention from abroad and by the fact that the U.S. government, claiming to be the leader of the free world, felt under some pressure to repair America's tarnished image.[71] This was one reason that some American conservatives, then and later, regarded the international liberal order with suspicion and as a threat to American sovereignty.

The same phenomenon of international socialization also played a role in the spread of democracy. The United States was neither a faithful nor a consistent supporter of democratic government around the world throughout the Cold War, or after. Although it actively promoted democracy in the strategic core—in Japan, Germany, and Western Europe in the early postwar years, and in Eastern Europe and other parts of Asia in the 1980s and 1990s—in large parts of the world and for much of the Cold War the United States was often indifferent to democracy, at best. Richard Nixon frankly regarded democracy as "not necessarily the best form of government for people in Asia, Africa, and Latin America," a view apparently shared by many Americans today.[72] Because Americans feared radicalism (communism during the Cold War; Islamism today) more than they opposed authoritarianism, they often supported ostensibly reliable dictators like the Shah of Iran and the Philippines' Ferdinand Marcos, or today, the rulers of Saudi Arabia, the United Arab Emirates, and Egypt. And on some occasions they acquiesced in the overthrow of democratic regimes deemed unreliable—Mohammad Mossadegh in Iran in 1953, Jacobo Arbenz in Guatemala in 1954, Salvador Allende in Chile in 1973, Mohamed Morsi in Egypt in 2013.

It was only in the late Cold War years, under Carter and Reagan, that the American government began to shift toward more consistent support of democracy. Partly it was for strategic reasons. The Reagan administration, rejecting the approach advocated by Jeane Kirkpatrick, ultimately decided that democratic governments were better bulwarks against radicalism than "friendly" dictators (a strategic lesson yet to be learned in the Middle East).[73] But partly it was because the ideological competition with the Soviet Union required greater consistency and less hypocrisy. What was the "free world" if it wasn't free? As Reagan discovered, it was harder to criticize the lack of democracy in communist countries while the United States was supporting tyrannical governments that also systematically suppressed freedom, sometimes more brutally than the communists. Thus the United States ultimately helped pull the rug out from under dictatorships it had long supported in the Philippines, South Korea, and Chile. During the late Cold War, the United States used its influence to block military coups in Honduras, Bolivia, El Salvador, Peru, and South Korea. Elsewhere it urged presidents not to prolong their stay in office beyond constitutional limits. This made a difference in helping sustain the explosion of democracy across the globe from the late 1970s through the early 1990s. The political scientist Samuel P. Huntington once estimated that over the course of about a decade and a half, U.S. support had been "critical to democratization in the Dominican Republic, Grenada, El Salvador, Guatemala, Honduras, Uruguay, Peru, Ecuador, Panama, and the Philippines."[74]

In the end, and even if not always with idealistic motives, Americans wound up creating a world unusually conducive to the spread of democracy. The foundations of the liberal world order laid in the 1940s and 1950s were the most critical contribution. The transformation of the once predatory dictatorships of Japan and Germany into anchors of liberal economic and political order may alone have been the greatest stimulus to the explosion of democracy of the past half century. It made Europe and East Asia, once the world's cockpits of nationalist confrontations, into zones of relative peace, prosperity, and stability. The decades-long peace in these two regions reduced one of the greatest obstacles to democracy: insecurity. Nations constantly preoccupied with defending themselves against attack generally produce strong central governments that seem better able to carry out an effective defense. Would-be autocrats have an easier time justifying their strongman rule when they can point to external or internal threats. It was no coincidence that democracy in the modern world flourished first and most steadily in two island powers, the United States and Great Britain, while nations surrounded on all sides by potential enemies (like Germany) or with ill-defined and indefensible borders (like Russia) had a more difficult time.[75] By providing a higher overall level of security in the decades after World War II, the United States and the liberal order created a cushion for young democracies that might not have survived in a more dangerous world.

The fact that the strongest power in the world was itself a democracy also shaped the behavior of others. Ever since the invention of liberal government, the international balance of power between the liberal governments and the autocracies has affected the political orientation of lesser powers. Liberal revolutions failed in Europe in 1848 when the autocratic powers of Austria and Russia wielded greater influence on the continent than the liberal powers of Britain and France. The number of democracies rose after the victory of the democratic allies in World War I and then dropped again as the United States and its former allies retreated and the fascist powers rose in the 1920s and 1930s. After World War II, fascism, which had been thriving in the 1930s, was almost nowhere to be found while both democracy and communism spread. The explosion of democracy that began in the late 1970s blossomed fully after 1989, as the Cold War competition wound down and the United States and its fellow democracies emerged as the dominant forces.

Notably, those nations that sought or depended on American power for their security were more likely to become democracies than those which looked to the Soviet Union or China for support. This was surely one reason why South Korea, Taiwan, West Germany, and a number of Latin American countries became democracies while East Germany,

North Korea, and Cuba did not. Or why Eastern and Central European nations that were not democracies when members of the Warsaw Pact became democracies when they had the opportunity to join NATO. In some cases democratization was the price of admission to the American security order, but in more cases it was simply a desire to conform to the norms of the liberal order where security was to be found. The strength of NATO, along with the relative prosperity of the leading democracies in the European Community, created incentives for others to join these increasingly successful clubs.

The overall effect was a radical departure from the course of history before 1945. Prior to World War II, democracy was in decline, and it had been virtually nonexistent over the previous five thousand years. After 1989 it became so widespread that many came to regard it as part of some natural human evolution. But it isn't. Democracy has been sustained throughout much of the world these past decades not because it has taken deep root in newly fertile soil. Democracy has spread and endured because it has been nurtured and supported: by the norms of the liberal order, by global pressures and inducements to conform to those norms, by the membership requirements of liberal institutions like the EU and NATO, by the fact that the liberal order has been the wealthiest part of the world, and by the security provided by the world's strongest power, which happens to be a democracy.

LIFE OUTSIDE THE ORDER: THE COLD WAR AND ITS END

During the decades we commonly associate with the Cold War, therefore, the most significant historical development was not the global struggle between the United States and the Soviet Union, which was not very different from past great-power confrontations going back to Athens and Sparta. It was the growing power and reach of the liberal world order that was historically unprecedented. The new liberal world order not only transformed international relations among its members, as well as their domestic politics and society. It also shaped the foreign and domestic behavior of those outside the order. It helped convince Soviet leaders to undertake reforms that led to the collapse of Soviet communism. Perhaps just as importantly, the revolutionary nature of the liberal order played a key part in bringing the Cold War to a peaceful end when other great-power confrontations throughout history had usually ended in war. The end of the global confrontation revealed the power and success of the liberal world order which had gone unnoticed in the heat and turmoil of the Cold War struggle.

There was nothing inevitable about the way the Cold War ended, either the fact of the Soviet collapse or the peaceful way it collapsed. From the 1930s through World War II and the early decades of the Cold War, Soviet communism had more than held its own as a force in the world. In the 1930s, when the capitalist democracies were staggering under 25 percent unemployment and many were questioning whether capitalism could survive, Stalin successfully industrialized the Soviet Union by channeling prodigious resources and manpower into heavy manufacturing.[76] Nor were the Soviets at any great geopolitical disadvantage in the looming global confrontation leading to world war. Lenin's prediction that the capitalists would destroy each other as they competed for imperial control of the world seemed more than borne out by both world wars, and the Soviet Union ultimately emerged from this period damaged but in a stronger position than it had enjoyed in a century. The courage and sacrifice of Soviet soldiers had beaten back the Nazis and left the Soviet Union in control of an Eastern European empire beyond anything achieved even by Peter the Great.

Communism also enjoyed a significant popular following around the world, even as Soviet citizens suffered under its many failings. After 1918 communist parties had appeared in over sixty countries on every continent.[77] Even Stalin's unprecedented murderous brutality—he killed more people through executions, forced collectivization, and the man-made famine in Ukraine than the Nazis did through the Final Solution—came during an era when violence and brutality had become the norm. In a postwar world wracked by poverty and suffering, the appeal of communism remained powerful. The first elections in Europe after World War II gave communist parties 26 percent of the vote in France, 38 percent in Czechoslovakia, 24 percent in Finland, and 19 percent in Italy.[78] In Asia, Mao Zedong was leading revolutionary forces in China, and other communist-led revolutionary movements were active in Vietnam, Indonesia, Burma, Malaya, and the Philippines.

In his secret "Long Telegram" in early 1946, George F. Kennan warned that as the debilitated European imperial powers retreated from their colonial holdings and independence movements sprang up, the Soviets would attempt to exploit the vacuum of power, employing "particularly violent efforts" to enhance "communist-Soviet penetration" and set up "Soviet-dominated puppet political machines" to take power when independence was achieved.[79] This prediction seemed borne out when the communists triumphed in China in 1949, North Korea invaded the South the following year, with Stalin's approval, and when the Marxist and nationalist Ho Chi Minh launched his effort to unite North and South Vietnam under communist rule. Considering where the Bolsheviks had begun in 1917, as a minority within a minority of revolutionaries, the Soviet Union by 1950 had achieved a stunning success.[80]

In retrospect, Americans may have somewhat exaggerated the risks communism posed to their "way of life" during the early Cold War, especially the threat of domestic subversion. But it is only from the comfort of a post–Cold War world, and with knowledge of the Cold War's outcome, that some can smugly disparage American concerns and declare the entire Cold War a "farce."[81] Every administration from Truman through Carter worried about the growing military power of the Soviet Union and about the growing challenge of communism in many parts of the world. Nor was the American perception of the Soviet communist threat appreciably different than that of the British, whose fear of "the communist danger" and determination to "withstand the Communist tide all over the world" significantly shaped Britain's policies toward the independence movements erupting across its empire.[82] Such generally unflappable and sober people as Kennan, Dean Acheson, and George Marshall, none of whom were inclined to regard the Soviet Union as a looming threat even as late as 1945, had begun sounding the alarm by 1946.[83] Looking at the rise of communist parties in Europe, State Department officials believed that a majority of European countries stood "on the very brink" and could be "pushed over at any time."[84] In his Long Telegram, Kennan warned that Soviet leaders were bent on the destruction of the United States and its "traditional way of life" and did not believe in any "permanent modus vivendi." To "cope with this force" would be the "greatest task our diplomacy has ever faced and probably [the] greatest it will ever have to face."[85] Ironically, it is only because the United States did take on that task, and for the most part did so effectively, that some could later argue that the Soviet Union never posed that much of a threat to begin with.

American officials feared the reach of Soviet power and the appeal of communism, but they did not regard either as invincible. It was Kennan's great insight that for all its genuine and apparent strengths, the Soviet communist system bore within it "the seeds of its own decay." He discerned that Stalin's apparent economic successes were built on a mirage and on the suffering of the Soviet people, which could not be sustained indefinitely. In any prolonged struggle with the combined economies of the United States, Western Europe, and Japan, the core of the liberal world order, the Soviet Union would prove to be "by far the weaker party." Kennan argued that a long and patient policy of containment would in time force the Soviets to turn in on themselves and face the internal contradictions of their society.

But that struggle had to be actively waged. As another strategic planning document, NSC-68, later put it, so long as the Soviet Union retained the initiative and remained "unchallenged by clearly superior counter-force," its vulnerabilities "would remain concealed by its successes."[86] Kennan argued that "Soviet pressure against the free institutions of the western world" had to be contained "by the adroit and vigilant application of counter-force at a series of constantly shifting geographical and political points" around the world. If the

Soviets encountered "strong resistance," Kennan believed, if their adversary possessed "sufficient force" and made clear "his readiness to use it," the Soviets would back off. If the United States and the democratic nations could be disciplined enough to carry out a policy of "long-term, patient but firm and vigilant containment of Russian expansive tendencies," then—but only then—would the inherent contradictions of Soviet communism "find their outlet in either the breakup or the gradual mellowing of Soviet power."

Containment was only one part of the equation, however. It was the prerequisite for the more important element of the strategy, which was protecting and strengthening the liberal order as originally conceived at the end of World War II. Even if Soviet expansion were contained, Kennan argued, everything would still depend on the "health and vigor of our own society." For it was the "palsied decrepitude of the capitalist world," the "fatalism and indifference" of the democracies to their own flaws, that had provided "the keystone of Communist philosophy." Kennan argued that it was up to the United States, in its new role as leader and protector of the new liberal world order, to harness the "self-confidence, discipline, morale and community spirit of our own people" and to provide other peoples around the world with a "positive and constructive picture of [the] sort of world we would like to see." The United States needed to look like a country that knew what it wanted, was able to cope with its domestic problems as well with "the responsibilities of a World Power," and which possessed a "spiritual vitality capable of holding its own among the major ideological currents of the time." Americans should be grateful for the challenge, Kennan believed, for it required "pulling themselves together and accepting the responsibilities of moral and political leadership that history plainly intended them to bear." It is a measure of how America has changed that such sentiments, if uttered today, would be greeted by snorts of derision by the realists of our time, by utopian determinists, and by those on the right and left who reject the very idea of responsibility and moral leadership.

It took longer than Kennan had hoped to force the Soviets to confront their weaknesses—he had predicted fifteen or twenty years. Partly this was because Soviet leaders enjoyed significant geopolitical successes throughout the first three decades of the Cold War, which distracted from and compensated for their domestic economic and political failings. The late 1940s and 1950s produced the successful communist revolution in China, the North Korean invasion of the South, the Soviets' successful test of a hydrogen bomb, the Suez Crisis and subsequent Soviet gains in the Middle East, and then the Sputnik launch, with its implications for Soviet missile technology. These successes gave Soviet leaders a measure of confidence, despite their increasingly serious economic problems and their objectively difficult strategic circumstances.

By the mid-1970s, the Soviet arms buildup under Brezhnev and Soviet gains in Africa, Latin America, and around the world gave both sides the impression that the "correlation of forces" was on the side of the Soviets—even though the Soviet economy in this same period was entering a death spiral. The Soviets also benefited from American failures, especially the failure in Vietnam, which produced divisions in the United States and helped convince Nixon and his national security adviser, Henry Kissinger, to discard the more confrontational aspects of containment in favor of détente and rapprochement—which the Soviets regarded as an American acknowledgment of weakness and decline.

It was not until the late 1970s and early 1980s, when détente was abandoned and American policy grew more confrontational again, that Soviet leaders finally came to fear that that they might not be able to keep up the geopolitical competition, and not just with the United States but with the liberal order more generally. The Americans made a remarkably quick turnaround from the Vietnam War—electing Ronald Reagan seven years after all U.S. troops had been pulled out and pursuing an arms buildup that began under Jimmy Carter and accelerated in the 1980s. Soviet setbacks in Afghanistan, the advent of Reagan's Strategic Defense Initiative, which Soviet strategists feared could negate their nuclear arsenal, all added to increasingly grave concerns about the state of the Soviet economy. Even before he took power, Mikhail Gorbachev believed the Soviets were "clearly losing the competition."[87] Facing what they regarded as the most hostile and aggressive U.S. administration since the early Cold War, Soviet leaders feared that if they could not gain a halt in the strategic and geopolitical confrontation, the Soviet Union by 2000 would be a "second-rate power."[88] Confronted by Reagan's refusal to compromise, Gorbachev told the Politburo, "We have no choice. We are . . . at the end of our tether."[89]

Great powers in the past, confronted by a similar set of circumstances, had armed and planned for war, and then sometimes launched war in order to improve their position while there was still time. Soviet leaders never even contemplated launching a war, partly because there was no attractive military option for improving their position or forestalling their relative decline. The American military commitment to its European allies had not wavered since the formation of NATO and was reinforced in the 1980s by its deployment of intermediate range nuclear weapons. The strength of the American nuclear arsenal, the buildup of its conventional forces, and the evident rededication of the U.S. government and people to aggressive prosecution of the Cold War limited Soviet options. In 1941 the Japanese could at least hope that the United States might give up the Philippines and its position in the Western Pacific rather than risk an all-out war. The Germans could hope in 1914 that Britain would not come to Belguim's defense. But the American guarantee to Europe in the 1980s seemed ironclad and, once again, geography worked in America's favor. Because the United States was so far away, even a successful Soviet invasion of Western Europe would not end the struggle. Even if the Soviet army marched across Europe, its most formidable adversary would remain untouched by war, with control of the oceans and vastly greater economic and industrial capacities, and with Asian allies to boot. Soviet leaders really only had two choices: continue on the path they had been on or undertake substantial domestic reforms to jump-start the economy and put the nation on a better footing either to compete or to seek an equitable truce.

The great success of the liberal order over the course of forty years played a critical role in Soviet calculations. In the days of Stalin and Nikita Khrushchev, the Soviets had been doing badly economically but not so badly compared to the capitalist nations. By the 1970s, however, the amazing recovery of Germany, Western Europe, and Japan cast in stark relief the weakness of the Soviets' economic system. By the 1980s, the relative economic position of the Soviet Union and its satellites was on a par with that of Latin America. Per capita GNP in the Soviet bloc fell to one-tenth of that in the developed capitalist world.[90] Given that the Soviets had always insisted on holding themselves to the liberal world's standards, and that Stalin and Khrushchev had promised to surpass the United States in various economic categories, these were demoralizing realities. The Soviet system was failing by its own measure.[91] As one German historian has observed, "the implosion of the Soviet bloc was a belated shattering of the illusions and self-deceptions that the leaders of the October Revolution had imposed on post-tsarist Russia, and which thereafter had been believed by generations of Communists the world over."[92] Gorbachev and his circle became convinced, as foreign policy adviser Anatoly Chernyaev put it, that Russians had to "leave our isolation and join the general flow of civilization."[93]

That remark in itself showed how much the world had changed and how much the success of the liberal world order had come to shape the perceptions of at least some Soviet leaders. No Soviet leader could have spoken of joining "the general flow of civilization" before 1945. What would that even have meant in, say, 1938? By the 1980s, the flow of civilization meant the rules-based, free trade economic system, the market economy and the welfare state, the liberal and humane norms, and the general peace and stability undergirded by American power and its system of voluntary alliances. In short, the liberal world order.

One of the first things to go as the Cold War approached its end was the Soviet alliance system. The fall of the Berlin Wall in 1989 symbolized both the Soviet system's collapse and the liberal order's success in changing the very nature of international relations. The Soviet Union, despite its radical ideology, practiced an old and very traditional brand of geopolitics. It ruled Eastern Europe much like a traditional empire. Nothing about the Warsaw Pact was voluntary, not the satellites' foreign policy nor their domestic political arrangements. "Everyone imposes his own system as far as his army can reach," Stalin had declared after World War II, and as a historical matter he was right.[94] That was the way it had always been. The peoples of Eastern and Central Europe had from the beginning been restive and resistant to Soviet domination. Refugees from East to West Germany alone averaged in the hundreds of thousands per year until the Berlin Wall was built in 1961 to stop the flow, and the Soviets had to use force to crush movements for reform and autonomy in East Germany, Hungary, and Czechoslovakia. But there was nothing new in that. By the standards of the world before 1945, and certainly by historical Russian standards, this was normal. In the nineteenth century, that high point of the "Westphalian order" celebrated by Kissinger and other realists, Metternich's Austria sent armies across borders to crush liberal revolutions in Italy and repress liberal movements in neighboring German principalities; France's restored Bourbon monarchy sent troops to put down anti-monarchical uprisings in Spain; and the Imperial Russian Army crushed rebellions in Poland. Beginning in the eighteenth century, Poland had been "partitioned" at least six times by Russia and other states, the last time by Stalin and Hitler in 1939. In the world before 1945, none of this was regarded as unusual, even if to some nineteenth- and early-twentieth-century liberal minds it had been objectionable.

In the liberal order erected after World War II, however,

Soviet behavior now appeared not only brutal but anachronistic. The Soviets were behaving normally in a world that was no longer normal. Peoples in the East could see that on the other side of the Iron Curtain no one was trying to escape and no one was being invaded. Alliances were voluntary, not coerced. By the late 1960s, even as Leonid Brezhnev proclaimed Moscow's right to use military force to keep its socialist allies in line, prominent Soviet officials were becoming embarrassed by their repeated interventions to put down reformist and autonomist revolts, and by what this said about the appeal of Soviet communism.

As part of his efforts to settle the Cold War and undertake needed reforms at home, and under heavy pressure from both the West and his own people, the last Soviet leader, Mikhail Gorbachev, allowed the Eastern and Central European states to break away from Soviet control. His successor, Boris Yeltsin, let even Ukraine and the other Soviet republics have their independence.[95] Among the most striking contrasts at the end of the Cold War were the different reactions of the two sets of allies. America's allies worried that the United States would withdraw its forces from Europe and return home. The members of the Warsaw Pact wanted to free themselves from the Soviet grip and worried about whether Moscow would ever truly let them go.

One factor is often ignored in accounts of the end of the Cold War: Gorbachev might not have taken such dramatic steps had he not believed it was safe to do so. According to his spokesman and biographer, Andrei Grachev, Gorbachev rejected Soviet propaganda about the threat from the West. Even with Reagan in power in the White House, Gorbachev did not believe the United States was "preparing to attack or invade the Soviet Union."[96] Clearly this was not only Gorbachev's perception; for as the Warsaw Pact countries drifted away at the end of the 1980s, even hard-liners in the Politburo had little to say about it. Not only was nothing done to prevent Poland, Hungary, Czechoslovakia, and others from pulling out, no senior Soviet official, including Gorbachev's opponents, suggested that anything should be done. Perhaps they believed it was too hard and risky to stop them, but they must also have believed it was safe to let them go, that the dismantling of this once vital strategic buffer would not imperil their nation's basic security.

One important reason was the change that had occurred in Germany, which had historically posed the greatest danger to Russia and the Soviet Union. Different German regimes had invaded Russia twice in less than thirty years, and the struggle between Teuton and Slav for control of Central and Eastern Europe went back centuries. After 1945 that threat had been removed, and four decades later Gorbachev and the Soviets preferred a unified Germany in NATO to an independent, neutral Germany. As Gorbachev told U.S. secretary of state James Baker, "We don't really want to see a replay of Versailles, where the Germans were able to arm themselves. . . . The best way to constrain that process is to ensure that Germany is contained within European structures."[97] Many Germans like to think they melted the East with friendliness, and perhaps they did, but a wealthy, armed, unified Germany, no matter how friendly, could not have made Russians feel safe had it not been anchored in an alliance that constrained its independent geopolitical ambitions.

This and other aspects of the liberal world order made it easier for Gorbachev to take such risks. In a normal competitive multipolar world, suing for an end to the competition and preemptively dismantling an empire meant endangering a nation's very survival, not to mention its continuance as an independent power. In the world created by the United States, however, it was possible for a great power to fall out of the competition and yet survive and even thrive. Germany and Japan had done it, and so had France and Britain and other European powers. They had all given up historic geopolitical ambitions in exchange for security, prosperity, and progress. Many Britons had regarded their centuries-old empire as part of their very identity as a people, and the loss of empire resonates even today. Yet Britons also took pride in their willingness to let it go. As one British historian has put it, "The civilised acceptance of a post-imperial role was the great enduring triumph of British history since 1945."[98] For a few years, it seemed that Russia might do the same. Gorbachev and Yeltsin both hoped to take a holiday from geopolitical competition, or perhaps to end it altogether, so that they might focus on their nation's economic and political health and lift the Russian people's standard of living to something closer to that of their Western neighbors. To do that did not require an empire. In fact, it required jettisoning the empire.

Because of the unusual circumstances that made it possible, the peaceful end of the Cold War was among the least inevitable events in history. Yet as often happens with historical events, we came to regard it as inevitable. Some historians and political scientists now insist that the Cold War was much ado about very little. They point to the Soviet Union's relative passivity during the Cold War, to the fact that it never invaded

Western Europe and never expanded beyond the territories taken in World War II. Soviet attempts to gain influence in Latin America, Africa, the Middle East, and Southeast Asia ultimately failed. One political scientist has even suggested that the United States ought to have let the Soviet Union expand farther, since its expansions only weakened it and drained resources.[99]

Yet if Soviet behavior proved to be more cautious and restrained than Americans anticipated, this was not due to some innate Soviet sense of restraint but to geopolitical realities, namely the strength of the United States and the liberal order. The American strategy of containment deterred some Soviet expansion and, where it didn't, helped make expansion too costly to succeed. Would an unfettered Stalin have shown the same restraint that he showed in the early years of the Cold War? Faced with a different set of circumstances and a more passive and accomodating American approach to the world, the Soviet Union would have behaved differently, as any great power would have. Had it not been confronted by "situations of strength" and "counterforce" everywhere it turned, it would have been stronger, more influential, and more expansive. If Soviet leaders had not witnessed the economic miracles of the liberal world order and had not also feared being outspent and out-innovated by the United States and its allies in a technological arms race, they might have believed that they could continue tinkering around the edges of their system rather than undertake the risky, regime-threatening reforms that ultimately undid the system. Had the United States and its allies not held together, based on their shared interest in the liberal world order, the Soviets would have found more fissures to exploit. Finally, had Gorbachev not believed it was safe to halt the strategic competition, and had Soviet leaders not regarded the liberal world as fundamentally unthreatening to their nation's basic security, they might have turned to conflict to forestall defeat or at least would have refused to enter a peaceful truce that left them permanently behind.

In the end, the threat of Soviet communism proved manageable, just as Kennan had predicted, but this was not because it never represented a genuine threat. It was because the United States pursued a grand strategy of creating and defending a liberal order that constrained Soviet ambitions and exposed its weaknesses as an economy, as a society, and as a world power.

THE STEEP PRICE OF SUCCESS

The cost of achieving this success was high. Nor were American officials in the postwar era under any illusions about the difficulty of the task. Walter Lippmann had immediately dubbed containment a "strategic monstrosity," mostly because he did not consider Americans up to the job.[100] They had not been accustomed to taking on vast global responsibilities at all, much less sustaining such a role over decades. Defending the liberal order meant operating in a gray area in which wars were fought not for victory but for less easily measured ends: stability, prosperity, progress, liberalism. Other peoples were not to be defeated but assisted, buoyed, given the tools and the protection to help themselves. In some cases they had to be converted. The conversions might begin as impositions but to be lasting had to become voluntary, as in Germany. Upholding and managing a liberal order was inherently difficult, therefore. For one thing, it had no end point. Pushing the jungle back from the garden is a never-ending task. There are no "mission accomplished" moments. Liberalism, prosperity, stability are constantly being eroded or undermined by enduring forces of habit and history and by enduring elements of human nature. Policies and policy formulations inevitably fell victim to the foibles common to all humans, no matter how well intentioned—the failures of insight and foresight, the selfishness and solipsism, and the overall incompetence endemic to all human activity. The result was, and had to be, repeated failure, frustration, and disillusionment, and for some that is a fair characterization of the Cold War—a disastrous jumble of paranoias and moral compromises, of excesses and miscalculations, of failures and follies.

Americans were certainly unready for the moral complexity of wielding such great power. They never reconciled themselves to the tragic reality that it was impossible to wield power, even in the best of causes, with clean hands. Americans liked to believe they were on the side of the good, but power is power and killing is killing, no matter how virtuous the objective. In every war, innocents are killed, dreadful mistakes waste the lives of brave soldiers, and even disciplined armies commit atrocities. It didn't matter to the civilians incinerated in Dresden or in Hiroshima that Americans thought they were fighting a righteous war against Hitler and Imperial Japan. What justified such horrors? Neither side in any conflict has a monopoly on truth and justice. Even a good cause has its selfish, venal side, and the adversaries have their own story to tell, a list of grievances by which they also justify their actions. Americans were shocked to learn this after World War I, when the Versailles settlement included territorial gains for the victors, and later when published archives revealed a more complex story of the origins of the war than Americans had understood. During the Cold War, the people and governments America supported were sometimes little better than the people it opposed—there were struggles between "half-angels" and "half-devils," as one of John le Carré's characters put it.[101] The unavoidable price of wielding power was to enter this moral no-man's-land. In taking on international "responsibilities," Americans lost what Reinhold Niebuhr called the "innocency of irresponsibility."[102]

Nowhere were the costs, both material and spiritual, higher than in Vietnam, where America's long and painful intervention proved that even smart and ultimately successful global strategies could produce tragic regional failures. Vietnam was certainly the product of containment—as later critics like David Halberstam maintained. The war may have proved to be a mistake, but it was not a misapplication of the doctrine. From the Truman administration onward, American leaders believed that the Indochina conflict was part of the overall pattern of violent communist expansion, an effort, as Kennan had predicted, to exploit anticolonial national liberation movements and turn them into communist revolutions. As late as 1965, Halberstam, along with the *New York Times* and *Washington Post* editorial pages, and members of Congress in both parties, believed it was both right and necessary for the United States to help the South Vietnamese resist aggression from the North and to protect them from the Soviet-style tyranny that would follow a Northern victory.

None of those basic assumptions was necessarily wrong. Two decades after the war ended, an editorial in *The Washington Post* reminded Americans of what most had by then forgotten: that the Cold War was not a "misunderstanding," that "there was such a thing as communism on the march," that it posed "a threat to what deserved to be called the free world," and that South Vietnam, "because it faced an armed takeover by an outside Communist regime . . . inevitably became a place where the confrontation was played out."[103] Like so much of American involvement both during and after the Cold War, it was not a fight for victory or conquest but, as one general put it, to restore "stability with the minimum of destruction, so that society and lawful government may proceed in an atmosphere of justice and order."[104] These were amorphous goals to be sending American soldiers to fight and die for, but they were not qualitatively different from the goals the United States had pursued in Europe and Japan or in Korea.

Could the United States have succeeded in Vietnam? If success meant the creation of an independent South Vietnam able to defend itself and thrive on its own, the answer was almost surely no. The only possible "success" would prob-ably have required Americans to do what they had done in Germany, Japan, and Korea, which was to provide the South Vietnamese protection for as long as necessary and maybe indefinitely. Those countries became success stories, key pil-lars of the liberal order that triumphed in the Cold War, and American forces remain there today, seven decades later. For a whole host of reasons, however, including the misguided strategy of the Vietnam War in the first four years of the con-flict, Americans had no interest in another such commitment.

The war left a difficult legacy. On the one hand, it destroyed, for a time, the tenuous consensus in favor of containment and America's global role. Many critics did not just turn against the war; they rejected containment and the whole trajectory of postwar American foreign policy. The war raised doubts not only about the rightness and morality of American foreign policy but about democracy, capitalism, and liberalism. Indeed, the effects of Vietnam on the American psyche were similar to the effects World War I had on an earlier generation and which the Iraq War would have thirty years later. Most of the critiques leveled at American foreign policy after the Cold War echo the major lines of criticism during and after Vietnam: that Americans had been led by ideologues on a quixotic and unachievable mission to transform the world; that this crusading idealism, if not curbed, would ultimately lead to the destruction of the nation, or the world; that the United States was in decline; that it had become, or always had been, a greedy, brutal, imperialist power, fighting endless wars against national liberation movements for the profit of the capitalists; and that Americans needed to show self-restraint, modesty, and humility, an awareness of the limits of power, and an acceptance of the world as it was, not as they wished it to be. In 1968 Noam Chomsky wrote that the United States had become "the most aggressive power in the world, the greatest threat to peace, to national self-determination, and to international cooperation."[105]

Even Henry Kissinger dissented from America's Cold War strategy as outlined by Kennan and Acheson. He did not believe the Soviet Union would collapse on its own contradictions. He insisted that Americans had to learn to live with the reality of Soviet power, possibly forever; that they had to accept the limits of their own power, and even their inevitable decline. He chided those who called for waging the Cold War vigorously, warning that it would lead to nuclear war. In the mid-1970s he declared that the theory behind containment, that it would "transform the Soviet Union," had proved to be a myth. The Soviets had only grown stronger and were impervious to outside pressures for change.[106] Efforts to seek strategic superiority and to apply pressure to the Soviet Union, the strategy of Truman and Acheson, were both futile and dangerous. Americans had to get used to the "imperative of coexistence."[107]

As early as 1968 Kissinger had believed the world was fast heading toward multipolarity, and he welcomed it. This author of a famous history of the early-nineteenth-century European balance of power believed a multipolar balance was more just and more stable than an order shaped by American predominance, which in any case was unsustainable. As Nixon put it in 1972, it would "be a safer world and a better world if we have a strong, healthy United States, Europe, Soviet Union, China, Japan, each balancing."[108] Kissinger even went so far as to assure the Chinese that the postwar structures the United States had created in East Asia would be dismantled. Keeping troops in South Korea, he told Chinese premier Zhou Enlai, was "not a permanent feature of our foreign policy"; Americans had been "extremely naïve" about Japan and regretted "how we built up Japan economically"; the Taiwan problem would go away. Once the two great powers came to agreement, he said the United States would not "stand in the way of basic evolution."[109]

Yet in spite of such despairing moments, despite the faltering and the failures, the pain of the wars, the fears of nuclear conflict, the societal divisions, the myriad critiques, and the partisan battles, the Cold War ended peacefully, almost exactly as Kennan had predicted. The successes of containment, it turned out, had been obscured by repeated crises and failures during those four decades, and they remain obscured today. But the fact was, Soviet expansion was prevented, the core elements of the liberal order endured and flourished, and Soviet leaders were forced to face the inadequacies of their system. The role of American power in all this was critical.

Had the United States chosen a different strategy— returning home, accepting multipolarity, putting its faith simply in international law and international institutions— history would have taken a different course. Instead, motivated largely by fear of communism, Americans accomplished a miracle without realizing it. The critics of American Cold War policies had predicted that the failures and follies, the paranoia and miscalculation, the excessive reliance on military power, the lack of accommodation, the failure to accept limits and the world "as it is," would lead either to Armageddon or to America's collapse from imperial overstretch or to the undermining of American democracy. Instead it led to an unprecedented era of peace and prosperity.

Could this remarkable success have been achieved without all the costs and failures, without the Vietnam War, the Bay of Pigs, McCarthyism, and all the other errors and evils associated with the American side in the Cold War? We will never know. We would of course like to think so. But we must consider the possibility that the price paid may have been unavoidable in a real world in which failure is as much a part of the human experience as success, that even successful strategies include error and disaster, that even the most improbably positive outcomes are not without their negative aspects. The strategy of containment and the grand strategy of support for a liberal order brought the United States into

Vietnam. It also led to the peaceful end of a global confrontation that would normally have ended in war, and in this case
possibly a nuclear war, but instead ended in peace.

THE "NEW WORLD ORDER"

After the collapse of Soviet communism, the world that
emerged was unlike any known in history. Within the liberal
world order, which by the end of the 1990s extended across
most of Europe and through much of Asia, Latin America,
and Africa, geopolitics had genuinely been replaced by geo-
economics. Among the great powers within the order, there
were no arms races, no militaries poised at borders, trade and
financial systems were relatively open, and most shared in a
historically unparalleled prosperity and unprecedented freedoms. It was a world symbolized by the European Union, a
"post-historical" institution where old nationalisms that had
brought so much strife to the world were submerged within
a new pan-European identity—long the dream of European
Enlightenment thinkers. Where once there had been only competition, there was cooperation. Where once there had been
tribalism, there was cosmopolitanism. Where once nations
fought for access to economic resources, now they were
bound together in mutual interdependence.

This was the world order that had evolved behind the
shield of containment. In the 1990s some called it a "new
world order," but it was not new. It was the world order
established after 1945, but with an expanded liberal Europe
and a diminished Russia in place of the Soviet Union. The
fundamental contours of the world had not changed. There

was still a Japan, a Germany, a Britain and France, a Russia, and a China. America still enjoyed its special advantages of geography and wealth. Many declared it a "unipolar" world, but the magnitude of the American role had not appreciably changed. People simply forgot that the order had not originally been conceived as a response to the Soviet Union but rather as a response to international and human realities that transcended any particular threat, and which still existed. Peace and progress had been made possible by the United States containing and suppressing geopolitical competition in the strategically most important regions of the world, by ensuring that the European powers and the Asian powers remained at peace, while guaranteeing the security of the great powers against each other. That did not end simply because one great power, Russia, had grown weaker relative to others. In Asia, nations still needed reassurance against a return of Japanese power and the rise of Chinese power, as well as against a North Korea seeking nuclear weapons. Nor had Russia ceased to have influence or the capacity to disrupt. Even in Europe, therefore, as the historian Geir Lundestad has noted, "the big surprise was *how little* the American role" had changed.[110] There was no call for American withdrawal but, on the contrary, anxiety to ensure that the United States remained fully engaged, politically, economically, and militarily. The NATO alliance not only persisted but European powers clung to it more tightly and the former Warsaw Pact members of Eastern and Central Europe scrambled to join it. When Germany reunified in 1991, only the promise that Germany would remain in NATO and that U.S. troops would remain on German soil calmed Germany's neighbors. Even France, which had sometimes regarded NATO as a tool of American hegemony, sought closer integration in the alliance.

Because the other "superpower" had weakened, the perceived "unipolar moment" led to concerns about an overbearing, "hegemonic," "arrogant" America lording it over others—the "hyperpower" as one French foreign minister put it in the late 1990s. But the United States had been plenty arrogant and overbearing throughout the Cold War.[111] It was no more or less so after the Soviet collapse. Moreover, whenever the United States showed signs of turning away from the world—as during the impeachment trial of President Clinton—suddenly many foreign leaders started worrying about what would happen if "Washington's gaze" became distracted. Liberal European newspapers took a break from denouncing America's "camouflaged neocolonialism" to note that "problems in the Middle East, in the Balkans or in Asia" could not be solved "without U.S. assistance." People who had been calling America "overbearing" were suddenly "praying for a quick end to the storm."[112]

The first two administrations of the post–Cold War era both believed that the United States still bore "international responsibilities." Although George H. W. Bush and Bill Clinton could not have been more different in many ways, including the fact that one was a Republican and the other a Democrat, they shared the belief that the United States still had to be the primary defender of a liberal world order—the "new world order," Bush called it. The United States was still the "indispensable nation," to use Clinton's famous phrase, which only echoed the sentiments of Dean Acheson decades before, when he had declared the United States the "locomotive at the head of mankind."[113] As former Clinton official Stephen Sestanovich observes, "The Clinton administration's steady revival of an activist U.S. role was based on policy premises that were identical to those on which the policy makers of the Truman administration began to wage the Cold War."[114] But since there was no Cold War to fight, it would be more accurate to say that both Bush and Clinton based their approach on the same principles as the strategy chosen before the onset of the Cold War in 1946.

The first test of the new era came when Saddam Hussein's Iraq invaded Kuwait in 1990. Bush's response was very much in keeping with the original grand strategy dating back to World War II. Failure to respond forcefully would set "a terrible precedent," Bush's adviser Brent Scowcroft believed, one that would only "accelerate violent centrifugal tendencies within the emerging 'post–Cold War' era."[115] Like Truman in Korea in 1950, Bush saw parallels with the 1930s—"I wanted no appeasement," he later wrote.[116] Like Roosevelt in 1940, he argued that "a world in which brutality and lawlessness" were "allowed to go unchecked" wasn't the kind of world Americans were going to want to live in.

Such thinking also informed Bush's decisions to intervene in Panama and Somalia, and Clinton's decisions to intervene in Haiti, Bosnia, Kosovo, and to launch an air and missile campaign against Iraq. When Bush sent thirty thousand troops to remove the corrupt Panamanian dictator Manuel Noriega, it was, as George Will wrote approvingly at the time, to fulfill "the rights and responsibilities that come with the possession of great power."[117] After the 1995 massacre at Srebrenica, Bosnia, Clinton officials argued that "Serb aggression" tore at "the very fabric of the West."[118] These minor interventions were all viewed by American officials as part of managing and defending the world order, although they also protected specific American interests: Bush reversed Iraq's aggression against Kuwait and kept control of the vast oil reserves of the Persian Gulf out of the hands of a serial aggressor. He removed a Panamanian dictator convicted of running a drug supply operation in the United States. Clinton restored a democratically elected Caribbean leader, thereby staunching the flow of tens of thousands of Haitian refugees to American shores. He twice acted to prevent genocide in the Balkans, after years of allied calls for help, and partly as a way of reaffirming America's commitment to European security. The only purely humanitarian intervention was in Somalia. That operation would ultimately be deemed a failure because of the tragic loss of eighteen American soldiers during a raid in Mogadishu on Clinton's watch. Forgotten, however, was that the American intervention, instigated largely under the direction of General Colin Powell, saved over 200,000 Somali lives.

This was not an "era of indiscriminate interventions" undertaken in a mood of "giddy optimism," as some would later assert.[119] None of these actions was taken without long reflection and tortured debate. Most were taken reluctantly, not eagerly. The United States went four years without addressing the crisis and the killings in the Balkans until Clinton, with his back against the wall, finally intervened to prevent a new round of ethnic cleansing and to force a diplomatic settlement. And most of these interventions were successful, by any reasonable measure of success, and were carried out with minimal cost by historical standards. There were no American combat losses at all in the Clinton administration's three interventions in Haiti, Bosnia, and Kosovo. There were remarkably few even in the 1991 Gulf War, though experts had predicted thousands of American soldiers would die. Altogether, fewer Americans died in combat in the entire decade of the 1990s than in every single month of the Vietnam War from 1966 to 1972. During the twelve years of Bush and Clinton, meanwhile, defense spending fell by 30 percent; the number of active duty military personnel dropped from over two million to 1.3 million; and the number of troops deployed overseas went from 453,000 to 210,000.[120] These were the lowest numbers since the 1930s.

Among the supposed "follies" of American foreign policy in those years—more evidence, allegedly, of American hubris and overreach—was the enlargement of NATO. According to critics at the time and later, the admission of Poland and other Central and Eastern European nations into NATO poisoned relations with Russia, prevented any accommodation, and gave rise in Russia to fears that its security was imperiled. We will turn in a moment to whether Russian anxieties could ever have been allayed, no matter how cautious and restrained American policies had been, but at the time the decision to bring the nations of Central and Eastern Europe into NATO was a response to *their* fears and anxieties. Given the long and consistent history of Russian intervention and imperial domination in Central and Eastern Europe, and especially the recent experience of the Cold War, the countries in that traditional Russian sphere of interest had reason for prudent concern. From very early on, Russia's neighbors worried that their newly won liberation from Soviet control might not last. As German sociologist Ralf Dahrendorf put it at the time, even Gorbachev's call for a "common European home" was not entirely comforting. There was "something suspicious about yesterday's hegemonic power wishing to set up house with those whom it occupied and held under its tutelage for so long."[121] German chancellor Helmut Kohl pushed German unification through as fast as he did in 1991 in part because he worried that Russia was just one coup away from reversing course.[122] By the mid-1990s, Eastern and Central Europeans had become so desperate to join NATO that even the more hesitant Western European powers like France came around to supporting the admission of at least some of them.

Whatever the effect on the Russians may have been, the enlargement of NATO brought stability, democracy, and prosperity to nations in Eastern and Central Europe that had rarely enjoyed any of those things. A Europe "whole and free" represented another sharp break from history and prevented that region from either descending into turmoil or becoming, once again, victim of a struggle between East and West. The benefits to world peace and stability were significant, and the costs to the United States were comparatively minor.

Success in world affairs has often proved its own undoing. In retrospect, it is clear the liberal world order began to erode at the very moment of its widely heralded triumph at the end of the Cold War. Partly this was due to the forces of history and human nature that never stopped exerting their influence, despite proclamations of the "end of history." And partly it was due to excessive optimism and complacency. Americans after the Cold War were disinclined to continue spending resources and taking the risks to resisit those forces as they had during the Cold War. Even as the post–Cold War administrations tried to minimize the costs and risks of upholding the liberal world order and to take a "peace dividend," the American public was restive. The end of the Cold War seemed to many an opportunity finally to lay down the burdens and responsibilities of preserving the liberal world order after four decades of heavy engagement. The "new world order," many believed, would sustain itself. People regarded the new era of peace and prosperity as a new normal, a new plateau of human existence in which geopolitics had actually ceased. The seminal "realist" thinker Hans Morgenthau once observed that Americans tended to look forward to the day when "the final curtain would fall and the game of power politics would no longer be played."[123] The end of the Cold War seemed to many to be that moment. The leading thinkers of the time all sounded like the theorists of global peace before World War I. Some claimed that advances of technology and economic globalization had created new iron laws that required autocracies to become democracies and great powers to pursue peace. Fukuyama and others predicted that the whole world was going the way of post–Cold War Europe toward a "post-ideological," "post-historical," " 'Common-Marketization' of international relations."[124] In this new era, American power seemed anachronistic. For some it was dangerous; for most it was simply expensive and superfluous.

Meanwhile, self-described realists warned of "imperial overstretch," insisting that America's global role outstripped its capacities. Realists had made this case in the 1930s and throughout the Cold War. After the Cold War, when the United States was arguably more powerful than ever, they returned to the old theme.

One early indication of this new mood was the response to drafts of a post–Cold War defense strategy produced by the Bush administration in 1992. The proposed strategy was essentially a continuation of the original grand strategy formulated during World War II, which had been adjusted to meet the challenge of the Soviet Union and international communism, but was always intended as a general strategy for dealing with the world and avoiding the catastrophes of the first half of the twentieth century. The 1992 Defense Planning Guidance called for the preservation of American primacy in world affairs, the strengthening and deepening of its democratic alliances, and continued support for international institutions and an open trading system. That year Samuel P. Huntington argued that "a world without U.S. primacy" would be "a world with more violence and disorder and less democracy and economic growth. . . . The sustained international primacy of the United States" was "central to the welfare and security of Americans and to the future of freedom, democracy, open economies, and international order in the world."[125] This was no more than what Dean Acheson would have said, and the draft strategy showed a remarkable continuity with the main thrust of American strategy over the previous forty-five years. Yet it was greeted in the press and by critics as a novel and appalling assertion of American global hegemony, a rejection, wrote *The New York Times*'s Patrick Tyler, of "collective internationalism."[126]

The reaction reflected a certain ignorance of what America's strategy had been since Acheson called the United States the "locomotive at the head of mankind." The world order had certainly not been constructed on the principle of "collective internationalism," unless one believed that the world was truly run by the United Nations in its pure, theoretical form. But equally clear from the reaction was the degree to which many Americans did not want to continue in such a role. They either believed it was no longer necessary for the United States to sustain a liberal world order, or that such an order no longer needed sustaining at all, that indeed, as Fukuyama claimed, the "End of History" had arrived. Whatever the explanation, many Americans were shocked to discover there were people in the government who still regarded American "primacy," as Huntington put it, as essential.

Indeed, with communism and the Soviet Union gone, even erstwhile conservative hawks joined in calling for a contraction of America's role in the world. In a September 1990 article entitled "A Normal Country in a Normal Time," former U.N. ambassador Jeane Kirkpatrick argued that there was no longer a need for sacrifice. The Cold War had given foreign policy "an unnatural importance" in American life. It was time for Americans to focus on their national interests as "conventionally conceived"—to protect their "territory, wealth, and access to necessary goods." That was the "normal condition for nations."[127]

Bush and Clinton thus found their continued efforts to defend the liberal world order attacked from all sides. Realists criticized them for acting where American "vital interests" were not at stake and engaging in "international social work." The left accused them of carrying out imperialist adventures in the interest of corporate profits—"no war for oil" was the cry when Bush turned back Saddam Hussein's aggression in Kuwait and when Clinton bombed suspected weapons of mass destruction facilities in Iraq in 1998. Votes on the interventions of the 1990s were highly partisan, with Democrats opposing Republican interventions and Republicans opposing Democratic interventions. "Don't bomb before breakfast" was the memorable suggestion of the old Cold Warrior Jack Kemp after the Clinton administration launched missile strikes in Iraq to prevent a massacre of the Kurds.

The lack of support affected American foreign policy in these years in ways that would later have profound consequences. Concerns about public opinion led Bush to end the war with Iraq after one hundred hours and before Saddam Hussein's Republican Guard had been destroyed. When Saddam then put down uprisings of Shi'a and Kurds, killing tens of thousands, the Bush administration, with troops just across the border, did nothing. Bush himself would later regret the resulting partial victory that left Saddam in power.[128] Concerns about public disapproval after Somalia helped convince the Clinton administration not to intervene to prevent one of the worst genocides in history in Rwanda; or to take military action against the then primitive North Korean nuclear program. Fear of public backlash also played a critical part in dissuading the Clinton administration from taking decisive action against al Qaeda bases in Afghanistan, where the 9/11 attacks were later prepared.[129] The result was that even in the relatively permissive strategic environment of the 1990s, the United States did not respond to significant and well-known threats that would later prove deadly, threats that would not have gone ignored during the Cold War.

And of course, that permissive environment did not last. Just as nascent liberal democratic governments in Japan and Germany in the 1920s had given way to authoritarian fascist regimes and more aggressive nationalist foreign policies in the 1930s, anticipated liberalizations in Russia and China did not play out as expected and, in Russia's case, gave way to a revanchist foreign policy to reestablish as much of the former Soviet Union and its sphere of influence as possible. In the Middle East and North Africa, a violent strain of radical Islam had grown in strength since the 1970s, seeking to reclaim the region from European colonial powers and the secular authoritarian governments the imperial powers had either imposed, supported, or tolerated. Inside the liberal order, progress continued to unfold, but outside the liberal order the deep patterns of history that were temporarily contained at the end of the Cold War began to reemerge.

The decade of the 2000s delivered a series of powerful blows both to the liberal order and to the United States, and the United States inflicted some on itself. The result was a substantial collapse of public support for the postwar grand strategy and a further weakening of the liberal order that strategy was designed to uphold.

The terrorist attacks on September 11, 2001, in which more Americans were killed on American soil than at any time since Pearl Harbor, led to an understandable panic about the threat of radical Islamic terrorism. The invasion of Afghanistan to remove al Qaeda bases and the Taliban regime that supported them, which the Clinton administration had shied away from in its last year, was launched. Then the Bush administration launched an invasion to remove Saddam Hussein from power in Iraq. The motives behind the first war seemed obvious—they were a response to the terrorist attack and an effort to prevent others. The motives behind the war in Iraq were more complicated. They were a blend of post-9/11 and pre-9/11 concerns.

Iraq in the 1990s had been principally a problem of world order management, albeit with elements of direct risk to the United States. The George H. W. Bush administration had bequeathed to the Clinton administration a wounded but defiant Saddam Hussein determined to get out from under the oppression of American power and extend his hegemony in the Middle East. Prior to his defeat in 1991, he had pursued those ambitions in wars with neighboring Iran and Kuwait and had launched programs to create nuclear, chemical, and biological weapons that would extend his power and make him immune to Iranian, Israeli, and American attack. His nuclear program was sufficiently advanced in 1981 to prompt an Israeli attack to destroy it, and at the end of the Gulf War in 1991, American intelligence agencies were shocked to discover that those programs had advanced further than they had suspected. The first Bush administration imposed an inspections regime to ensure they were destroyed, but over the course of the 1990s Saddam did his best to inhibit the inspectors' work, and in 1998 he had thrown the inspectors out, prompting the Clinton administration to launch a four-day campaign of bombing and missile strikes on suspected facilities. Thereafter, American intelligence was essentially blind, unable to determine exactly what programs Saddam possessed and how far along they were. Instead, the intelligence community had been forced to speculate. In retrospect, it appears that having earlier erred in underestimating the extent of Iraq's programs, they now erred in overestimating them. In 2000 the Clinton CIA produced two reports warning that Iraq was "steadily producing WMD capabilities," and Saddam himself made every effort to portray his programs, including his nuclear weapons program, as further advanced than they turned out to be, presumably to deter the Americans, Iran, and even his own people from moving against him.[130]

President Clinton and his top advisers regarded the threat posed by Saddam Hussein much as the first Bush administration had, not primarily as a threat to the United States but to the world order they hoped to uphold after the Cold War. Clinton told Americans in 1998 that it was a matter of "remembering the past and imagining the future." The post–Cold War era had opened remarkable new opportunities for economic, technological, and political progress. The "superpower confrontation ha[d] ended." Yet it was "not a time free from peril." Privately, he told his aides that "in the aftermath of the Cold War," it turned out that "every good thing" had "an explosive underbelly."[131] Publicly, he sounded themes similar to FDR's in 1937. The post–Cold War world, he warned, contained "outlaw nations and an unholy axis of terrorists, drug traffickers, and organized international criminals," "predators of the twenty-first century" who fed "on the flow of information and technology." If the United States and the liberal world did not prevent them from building "arsenals of nuclear, chemical, and biological weapons and the missiles to deliver them," they would become "all the more lethal." Iraq was only the beginning. The coming century was likely to see "more and more of the very kind of threat Iraq poses— a rogue state with weapons of mass destruction ready to use them or provide them to terrorists." If the United States and others failed to respond, "Saddam and all those who would follow in his footsteps" would be emboldened "by the knowledge that they can act with impunity."[132]

These were Clinton's arguments in 1998 when he ordered the four-day bombing of Iraq's suspected weapons production sites. That limited action was an indication of the pressures the administration was under not to commit the United States to a major military operation, and indeed, the day after the speech, his top advisers were shouted down at Ohio

State University with chants of "One, two, three, four! We don't want your racist war," and Republicans later came out against the bombing, charging that Clinton was trying to distract attention from the Monica Lewinsky scandal.[133] When the administration of George W. Bush made the case for war against Iraq in 2002, however, his arguments were essentially the same as Clinton's.

The difference was that in the post-9/11 environment, fear in the United States was much higher, and actions that had been unthinkable before became thinkable. There was no evident link between Iraq and the September 11 al Qaeda attack, but there were al Qaeda fighters in Iraq, including one of Osama bin Laden's top lieutenants. The Bush administration saw the possible conjunction between terrorism and weapons of mass destruction as a serious threat, just as the Clinton administration had before, and as did many Democrats, and as did many Americans. Although the circumstances were different, Bush's broad rationale for war was the same as his father's rationale a decade earlier. His arguments focused on American security but also on the state of the world. He would not "allow a nation like Iraq, run by Saddam Hussein, to develop weapons of mass destruction and then team up with terrorist organizations so they can blackmail the world."[134] This was a popular view at that moment. The effect of the 9/11 attacks had been to lower Americans' tolerance for the kind of threat Saddam posed and increase the price they were willing to pay to eliminate it. Al Gore in 2002 said Iraq was "a virulent threat in a class by itself," and even liberals like Christopher Dodd, Harry Reid, and Tom Harkin voted to authorize war.[135] As Hillary Clinton observed in casting her vote for the war in 2002, "In balancing the risks of action versus inaction, I think New Yorkers who have gone through the fires of hell may be more attuned to the risk of not acting."[136] For a moment, sins of omission loomed larger than sins of commission.

That moment did not last. The Iraq War resembled the Vietnam War in many ways. As with Vietnam, the war followed naturally from a foreign policy doctrine that successive administrations had embraced and justified. Like Vietnam, it enjoyed significant support initially—the Senate voted 77–23 to authorize the Iraq War, with 29 out of 50 Democrats voting in favor. This reflected polls that showed large majorities in favor of the war—and the war remained popular even after initial setbacks, including the failure to discover suspected WMD stockpiles.[137] As with Vietnam, support faded only as it became increasingly clear that the U.S. military was bogged down in a seemingly endless and possibly losing effort. As in Vietnam, the United States did not seek conquest but hoped to turn Iraq over to the Iraqi people as quickly as possible. As in Vietnam, American political and military strategy proved inadequate to the task. The failures of those early years so undermined public support for the war that by the time a new general devised a successful political-military strategy it was too late to reverse the downward spiral of support in the United States. As in Vietnam, the faulty intelligence regarding Iraq's weapons of mass destruction programs led to charges that officials had not merely been mistaken in their assessment but had lied. In time the entire war came to be viewed by many as a deliberate deception by the government.

As with Vietnam, many of those who turned against the war they once supported also turned against the entire foreign policy doctrine they once supported. In the same way that the foreign policy elite of the Democratic Party reversed itself and collapsed after Vietnam, so the bipartisan foreign policy elite that had supported the Iraq War reversed itself and imploded. Some of the war's biggest supporters became its most visceral retrospective critics. When the damage from the war was then compounded by the onset of the Great Recession of 2008, the bottom fell out.

By the time of the 2008 election, post–Cold War optimism had given way to a deep national pessimism. A new "realism" came into vogue, the conviction that the world was intractable, that the United States simply lacked the power to shape it effectively, and that rather than fix things the employment of American power only made things worse. Many argued that the United States had created most of the world's problems through its misadventures and that Americans would be better off letting the world take care of itself. Disillusionment combined with a sense of futility. Things might be bad out there, many Americans came to believe, but American intervention was likely either to be ineffective or to make them worse. As an indictment of American power, this new realism was reminiscent of the post-Vietnam 1970s, but as a prescription and an attitude about America's proper role in the world, it more resembled the 1920s and 1930s. Without the Cold War confrontation, the conviction grew that what happened in the world didn't matter very much. That made the errors and costs of American actions all the more unforgivable.

This shift in American attitudes, although it began long before the Iraq War, explains why the Iraq War has had such a deep and lasting impact on American attitudes toward foreign policy and America's role in the world. The failure alone does not suffice to explain the reaction. As costly as the Iraq War was, it didn't compare to previous wars. More than 33,000 American soldiers died in three years of fighting in Korea. The United States lost ten times as many soldiers in Vietnam as it did in Iraq—indeed, from 1966 to 1971 there were more Americans killed in Vietnam every year than in all eight years of fighting in Iraq. In the Vietnam era, society was more deeply polarized. Violence and unrest rippled across the country. A president was forced to resign, and the nation slid into the worst economic crisis since the Second World War, partly as a consequence of the war. Yet four years after the North Vietnamese invasion and final conquest of the South, even the administration of Jimmy Carter was turning hawkish, increasing the defense budget, arming anti-Soviet fighters in Afghanistan, and retargeting American nuclear forces to increase their "war-fighting" capability. Then in 1980 the country elected the most hawkish Cold Warrior since Truman. Fear of the ideological and strategic threat posed by Soviet communism was enough to sustain the American public even after the failure of Vietnam.

The trajectory of the United States after Iraq has been different. The pessimism and calls for retrenchment and disengagement have continued for more than a decade, and with no end in sight. This cannot be attributed only to the failures of Iraq and Afghanistan, even compounded by the effects of the 2008 financial crisis and the recession that followed. Rather, it is due to the widespread conviction that the role the United States has been playing in the world for the past seven decades is no longer necessary, perhaps was never necessary, and in any case no longer serves American interests. Americans' tolerance for the inevitable failures of foreign policy and war is largely a function of the dangers they perceive in the world. American involvement in World War II began with a series of disasters in the Philippines and North Africa that cost tens of thousands of lives in a few months, yet those losses did not undermine American support for the war against Japan and Germany, even among Americans who had opposed intervention just a year earlier. Nor did the Vietnam War ultimately undermine support for the strategy of containment and vigorous prosecution of the Cold War. Yet when four soldiers were killed in October 2017 in special operations against Islamic terrorists in Africa, the *New York Times* editorial page wondered "how many new military adventures" the public would tolerate and suggested it was "time to take stock of how broadly American forces are already committed to far-flung regions and to begin thinking hard about how much of that investment is necessary."[138] With no Soviet Union or international communism to fight but only a liberal world order to protect against various and sundry threats, Americans increasingly did not see the point. The threats didn't seem worth the price.

The election of Barack Obama in 2008 was a watershed in this regard. Obama came to office with a popular mandate to restore something closer to normalcy to American foreign policy. A critic of American power and its excesses during the Cold War, he shared the post–Cold War orthodoxy that America's extensive interventionist role in the world had become unnecessary, unsustainable, and counterproductive. He set out to reposition the United States in a more modest role appropriate to a new era of global convergence. Viewing the contested world of the Cold War as a relic, he sought accommodation with old adversaries and competitors in Moscow, Tehran, and Havana, while seeking to lessen the burdens of America's responsibility to allies. He also carried out his campaign promise and withdrew all American forces from Iraq. He increased force levels in Afghanistan, but with a tight deadline for their reduction, which mitigated their impact.

When Obama did try to uphold the liberal world order, moreover, he was often attacked by Republicans. Many criticized him for intervening in Libya, and when he walked up to the precipice of military action in Syria, they made clear their opposition, just as they had with Clinton's interventions in the 1990s. This could only have deepened Obama's conviction that Americans no longer favored the old active role. And so beginning two years into his presidency, and even as the liberal world order began to show further signs of strain and cracking around the edges, Obama did what the American people evidently wanted, which was very little. When Russia invaded Ukraine and seized the Crimean Peninsula, the only act of territorial aggression in Europe since the Second World War, he limited his response to economic sanctions. He rejected providing even defensive weapons to Ukraine, partly on the grounds that Ukraine was within Russia's sphere of influence. As the Arab Spring rose and fell, when the situation in Libya deteriorated, when turmoil erupted in Egypt, war began in Yemen, and a deadly new terrorist organization established control of a wide swath of territory straddling the Syrian-Iraqi border, the Obama administration initially limited its response to drone strikes and small Special Forces operations. As the Syrian conflict metastasized, killing hundreds of thousands and sending millions more as refugees into Europe, helping to send that continent into its worst political crisis in decades, the administration increased forces on the ground but never with the intention of forcing a peaceful settlement in Syria. As the killing and refugee flows continued, and even as Russia and Iran became more deeply involved with their own forces, Obama remained determined to avoid a substantial commitment of American power. The American public was indifferent. In rejecting the course of previous administrations, Obama did what the majority of Americans wanted.

If there was any doubt about that, the 2016 election ended it. There were four major political figures on the national stage that year: Obama, Bernie Sanders, Donald Trump, and Hillary Clinton. Only one of them stood for the old grand strategy—the other three were critics, from the left, the right, and the center-left. Clinton, the last national spokesperson for the "indispensable nation" and the liberal world order, was isolated and so much on the defensive that she turned against her own signature accomplishment as secretary of state, the Trans-Pacific Partnership trade agreement (TPP) negotiated among eleven nations, including such key American allies as Japan and Australia. The election of 2016 was a repudiation of the old strategy, and not because of Donald Trump. He was the beneficiary of the national mood. The mere fact that Americans could elect someone with so little government experience, and no foreign policy experience at all, showed how little they cared about America's role in the world. If anything, they responded favorably to Trump's denigration of the liberal world order and America's role in supporting it. Even if Clinton had won, it is questionable whether she could have bucked this prevailing mood, much less changed it. If Franklin Roosevelt couldn't do it in the 1930s, could Hillary Clinton have done it today?

. . .

So that is where we are. The popular and political consensus behind the old grand strategy has collapsed. A new consensus has emerged across the political spectrum, from left to right, from Main Street to Wall Street, from Trump supporters and conservative Trump opponents to former Obama officials, supporters of Bernie Sanders, and repentant members of the "foreign policy elite." Believing that the last quarter century of American foreign policy was a disaster, this consensus view calls for restraint and retrenchment. Critics argue that the United States has been engaged in a hubristic effort to shape the world in America's image, with foolish attempts to implant democracy in nations where no natural foundation for it exists, a refusal to respect other great powers' historical spheres of interest, and a general failure to recognize the limits of American power. In trying to accomplish too much, they argue, American policies these past three decades have actually damaged American interests and alienated average Americans. This is the view of a large segment of the Democratic Party, represented by Sanders and Elizabeth Warren, and it is the view of a large segment of the Republican Party, represented by the supporters of Donald Trump, Rand Paul, and even many who used to be called mainstream, establishment Republicans who have become dubious about both the possibility and the desirability of the liberal world order. They believe, as Obama administration officials put it when they came to office, that Americans need to accept the world as it is, not as they might wish it to be.

. . .

The problem is that we have lived inside the bubble of the liberal world order so long that we have forgotten what that world "as it is" really looks like. The critics who insist that the last quarter century of American foreign policy has been a disaster evidently have short memories. Which quarter century over the last hundred years would they like better? The first quarter of the last century included World War I and the birth of communism and fascism. The second quarter century saw the rise of Hitler and Stalin, the Ukrainian famine, the Holocaust, World War II, and the invention and use of nuclear weapons. The third saw the Cold War, the Korean War, the Vietnam War, McCarthyism, the Cuban Missile Crisis, and the Iranian Revolution. Even if the last twenty-five to thirty years have seen their share of failures, they have been characterized by great-power peace, a rising global GDP, and widespread democracy. A true realist would recognize that however problematic the last twenty-five years have been, on our current trajectory we are likely to see much worse.

THE RETURN OF HISTORY

There are signs all around us today that the jungle is growing back. History is returning. Nations are reverting to old habits and traditions. This should not be a surprise. Those habits and traditions are shaped by powerful forces: an unchanging geography, shared history and experiences, and often by spiritual and ideological beliefs that defy modern reason. Peoples and nations tend to revert to type. The Russia of today is different from the Russia of 1958 or 1918 or 1818, but it is also remarkable how much Russians' geopolitical ambitions and insecurities, their ambivalent attitudes toward Europe and the West, and even their politics have not changed. No one doubts that China's past, both its long regional hegemony in past centuries and its "century of humiliation" beginning in the early nineteenth century, shapes present Chinese attitudes, just as Iranians' ambitions are shaped by their Islamic and their Persian roots. We are always looking for and anticipating radical shifts in the trajectories of nations, but those shifts rarely prove as dramatic as we expect. Not so long ago people were talking about the remarkable rise of the BRICS, which, in addition to India and China, included the growing economic and political clout of Brazil and the economic success of Turkey, South Africa, and Russia. But today, aside from China and India, that phenomenon is already a thing of the past. Brazil has become Brazil again; South Africa has been mired in corruption and political turmoil; Russia has returned to being Russia. China has an emperor again. They have sunk back into old political, social, and economic habits.

This is true even in the heart of the West. In "post-historical" Europe, the past is not forgotten but lurks always just beneath the surface. It doesn't take much for Italians or Greeks to start calling Germans Nazis, for the French to joke about Germans marching down the Champs-Élysées, for Poles to feel nervously squeezed between their two historical conquerors. Many were surprised at the British vote to leave the European Union, but from a historical perspective there was nothing unusual about the English seeking distance from the continent. And the same holds for Americans. Their attitudes toward themselves and toward the world are still heavily shaped by the two vast oceans that stand between them and the world's other great powers. The fact that planes and ships and missiles, as well as digital signals, cross those oceans in a way they did not in previous centuries does not seem to have disturbed Americans' comforting belief that the world's problems need not affect them and that they have a choice whether or not to have a foreign policy. Hence Americans have also returned to old habits. History does not repeat itself, but nations travel along deep and broad ruts in which they have been traveling for hundreds of years, and though they may be knocked or pulled out of those ruts by powerful forces and events, there will always be a tendency to slip back into them. *Eadem, sed aliter* was Schopenhauer's phrase, "the same, but different."

We can't see the world "as it is" by looking at the world of the past thirty years, therefore. That world was shaped by American power and by the liberal world order to which other nations have been forced to adjust their behavior. Russia's behavior has been shaped by what Russian leaders believed the United States would or had to tolerate as well as by their sense of the liberal order's strength and cohesion. The same has been true of China's behavior, and Iran's, and that of every other nation or nonstate actor that might seek to disrupt or topple the existing order. All would behave differently if America behaved differently, and so would America's allies and the rest of the world. To see the world "as it is" requires imagining what the world would look like had history not been redirected by the United States, a world in which great powers returned to the paths they had been on before the United States stepped into its role. This requires no great feat of prognostication. It mostly requires remembering how nations have historically behaved when given the chance.

Russia's behavior has certainly conformed in recent years

to the long sweep of Russian history. For a brief moment, Russians toyed with breaking from their past, pulling out of the deep ruts, and redefining their interests, as Germany and Japan had been forced to do after World War II and as France and Britain did somewhat more voluntarily. The Russians seemed prepared to embrace integration in the American-led world order in order to reform, "modernize," and achieve prosperity—and also security—even if it meant abandoning centuries-old geopolitical ambitions, letting go of centuries-old insecurities, and giving up their historical sphere of interest.

That Russians ultimately rejected that course has been unfortunate but not entirely surprising. Nor was Russia's behavior primarily a response to actions by the West, such as the enlargement of NATO. Long-standing Russian ambitions and insecurities, together with a tradition of autocrats benefiting from popular fears of foreign threats, have made it difficult for Russia to steer out of old ruts.

For the better part of three centuries, the Russian empire had included everything from the territories of the Baltics to the Black Sea, as well as parts of Poland. For decades the Soviet Union was regarded by the world as a superpower, the equal of the United States, the co-manager of a "bipolar world." The Cold War may have been a low point for the living standards and individual freedoms of many Russians, but it was a high point in Russia's long history as a great power and empire, equaling the triumph of 1814 when Russian forces drove across Europe and occupied Paris. During the Cold War, pride in this superpower role even offered some compensation for the privations and abuses Russians suffered at home. If Russians had changed their historical trajectory after the end of the Cold War, if like Germany and Japan they had chosen economic over geopolitical competition, focused on improving their standard of living and integrating themselves fully into the liberal world economy, they might have lived better lives but at the price of Russia's historical greatness on the world stage.

We would like to believe that ordinary Russian people would gladly have traded superpower status for a freer, safer, and more prosperous existence. That is part of our modern, liberal faith. But the Russian people's desire to restore their country to greatness on the world stage proved to be a significant factor in Russian politics after the Cold War. Ultranationalists like Vladimir Zhirinovsky consistently received a quarter of the votes in elections, and Zhirinovsky's platform had less to do with national security, strictly speaking, than with national honor, national greatness, and the survival of Russian culture. "Unless we get back the historical borders of Russia," he argued, the Russian people were "slowly going to degrade and die out." The U.S. bombing of Serbia in March 1999 outraged Russians, not only because they sympathized with their fellow Slavs but because Russia's inability to do anything about it was a reminder of Russia's diminished stature on the world stage. Even the billions of dollars in financial aid provided by the West was humiliating. In the 1930s Stalin had promised, "We shall catch up to America and overtake it." Now America was giving Russia handouts.[139]

It did not help that the political and economic reforms instituted first by Mikhail Gorbachev and then by Boris Yeltsin neither improved Russians' economic situation nor, it seemed, produced true democracy. Instead, a few got rich and powerful while the rest suffered. The United States and the

West ended up providing Russia billions of dollars, but there were critical moments, including at the very beginning, when the Bush administration had been parsimonious. There was no Marshall Plan for Russia as there had been for Western Europe. It's not clear that it would have made a difference. The Russians had their own *Dolchstosslegende*, a Russian version of post–World I Germany's stab-in-the-back story, featuring Gorbachev and Yeltsin as the villains who caved in to the West, gave up Russia's position in Eastern and Central Europe, and allowed the Soviet Union itself to break up—the greatest "geopolitical catastrophe" of the twentieth century, as Putin put it.

It was in this context that the United States and the West came to be viewed as a threat: not to Russia's security but to Russian ambition and Russian pride. Many Russians, led by Putin, have pointed to NATO enlargement as proof of the West's hostile intent—and many American critics of the decision have agreed. But as Russian generals and strategic thinkers admitted in candid moments, NATO's expansion did not increase the alliance's overall military capabilities or the threat to Russian security. The two decades after the Cold War saw steady decreases in the numbers of U.S. troops in Europe and, even by Russian estimates, an overall reduction of the "joint military potential of its members."[140] Putin certainly had much less reason to worry about the U.S. or NATO threat when Barack Obama was in the White House than Gorbachev did in the era of the Reagan defense buildup. More than Russia's security, NATO's enlargement threatened Russia's ability to reassert its regional sphere of interest, to reclaim its position as a dominant power in Eastern and Central Europe and its standing on the world stage as an equal of the United States.

This may not have been strictly rational, but feelings of pride and honor are often more potent than rational calculations of interest. They shaped the policies of Germany and Japan, the self-described "have-not" nations of the late nineteenth and twentieth centuries, and the result was to create self-fulfilling prophecies. Germany's arms buildup accompanied by a bullying diplomacy produced the very predicament German leaders claimed to fear: the encirclement by hostile neighbors. Russia's actions have had the same effect. By the end of the Obama administration, Putin's attempts to restore Russian influence and military involvement from Northern Europe to the Middle East sufficiently unnerved its neighbors that the United States felt compelled to increase its military role in a region from which it had been steadily pulling away. Last year American forces in Eastern Europe increased for the first time in three decades.

Many in the West have seen this as a "security dilemma" and sought ways to solve what they regard as an unfortunate misunderstanding. Such was the theory behind the Obama administration effort to "reset" relations with Russia back in 2009. That effort failed, however, and in large part because it misdiagnosed Russians' feelings and motives. In the classic security dilemma as imagined by international relations theorists, insecurity rises on both sides despite the fact that both sides are trying to reduce their insecurity. Tensions rise even as both sides seek to reduce tensions. Yet reducing tensions has never been Putin's objective. He has wanted to increase tensions, and insecurity, on both sides. And he has had sound reasons for wanting to do so.

The problem Russia has faced since the end of the Cold War is that the greatness Putin and many Russians seek cannot be achieved in a world that is secure and stable, in which the liberal order remains coherent and cohesive, especially in Europe, and in which the United States remains willing and able to continue providing the basic guarantees that make the liberal order possible. Russia's economy today is the size of Spain's. Its military, except for its nuclear force, is no longer that of a superpower. Its demographic trends suggest a nation in decline. The present world order affords Russia the chance to be more secure than at any time in its history. But in this world order Russia cannot be a superpower. To achieve greatness on the world stage, Russia must bring the world back to a past when neither Russians nor anyone else enjoyed security. To return Russia to its historical influence on the world stage, the liberal order must be weakened and toppled, and international strategic competition must be returned to its normal historical state.

Such a world not only offers the best chance of restoring Russian greatness. It also serves Putin's personal ambitions. It justifies and even requires a strong leader. Like the tsars of the past, Putin tells the Russian people that to defend a "vast territory" and to occupy "a major place in world affairs" require "enormous sacrifices and privations on the part of our people."[141] Stalin said much the same, and indeed Putin's repeated comparisons of the United States with Nazi Germany and his claim that opponents in Ukraine and elsewhere are Nazis, evokes not only the Great Patriotic War and past Russian glory but also the need for a strong leader like Stalin.

Putin's hostility to the liberal world is also personal. Ever since he consolidated power, he has worried that the external forces of liberalism would work to undermine his authoritarian rule at home. Behind every democratic revolution on former Soviet territory, in Georgia, Ukraine, and Kyrgyzstan, he saw the hand of the West, and particularly the United States, even though the role of outsiders was not the decisive factor in the toppling of the authoritarian regimes in those countries. His objection to the expansion of NATO has less to do with the eastward advance of the alliance's military power than the presence of democracies closer to Russia's borders. Putin is at least as worried about the eastward advance of the European Union as he is about NATO. It was after Ukraine negotiated a trade agreement with the EU that he invaded and seized Crimea.

It is hard to see what concessions the United States and the West could offer to address the complex mix of feelings and motives whose sources are more internal than external, more psychological than strategic. Obama's "reset," his decision to trim back missile defenses in Poland in response to Russian objections, his tepid response to the attack on Ukraine, and his acceptance of a Russian military role in Syria and the broader Middle East did nothing to cure Russians' sense of grievance or tame Putin's ambitions. They only emboldened Putin to press for more. The election of Trump, who throughout his campaign expressed a desire for improved relations with Moscow, did not affect Putin's approach to the world. Those who suggest we should recognize a Russian sphere of interest in its region should recall that Russia's historical sphere of interest does not end in Ukraine; it begins in Ukraine. It includes the Baltic states, and it includes Poland.

That is a dangerous path to head down, as history has shown. Even if we sacrificed Ukrainian independence or Georgian independence or Baltic independence in the hope of calming Russian anxieties and sating Russians' ambitions, such concessions would not solve the problem, any more than feeding Manchuria to Japan and Czechoslovakia to Nazi Germany solved those problems. The peace established after World War II and which endures almost seventy-five years later was not based on accommodating Japanese and German anxieties, even though those nations suffered infinitely greater horrors at the hands of the Allies than anything Russians suffered at the end of the Cold War. Among the liberal order's greatest contributions to international peace has been the discrediting and denial of great-power spheres of interest. To begin acknowledging and accepting such spheres again would be a big step back to old patterns of history and to the conflicts and instability that characterize the international system "as it is."

Unfortunately, the liberal order has become sufficiently frayed, and the American role in the world sufficiently uncertain, that Putin is bound to continue probing for weaknesses. Until now Putin has sought to disrupt, divide, and degrade the liberal world order through murky actions in the gray area between war and peace—through half invasions, frozen conflicts, "little green men," and the manipulation of the Internet and social media, including interference in elections on both sides of the Atlantic. Whether he turns to more open forms of aggression in the future, against Ukraine again or even against a NATO ally like Estonia, will depend on his reading of the United States and the state of the liberal world order. If the order is strong and confident and backed by reliable American power, he will be cautious. A losing confrontation with the West could be embarrassing and loosen Putin's grip on power at home.[142] If the order appears weak and divided, however, and the United States appears uncertain or uninterested, he will be tempted to take the next bolder step. Nothing would more surely destroy the liberal order and put Russia back in the big game than proof that the United States was not prepared to come to the defense of a treaty ally in Europe.

An American president will face a frightening choice if Putin decides to test the system. Economic sanctions alone will be no answer to an attack on a treaty ally, even a murky attack in the gray area, but to do more, to employ NATO conventional forces, will quickly bring Russia and the United States, two nuclear powers, to the ultimate confrontation. Putin is already using nuclear threats to try to intimidate the United States and Europe. If the United States is prepared to go eyeball-to-eyeball again, as Kennedy did with Khrushchev in 1962, Putin will likely back down. But would an American president have the courage and the understanding to make him back down? President Obama said he didn't want to risk a nuclear war over Ukraine, but one is tempted to ask: Over which foreign country would he have been willing to risk nuclear war? If the United States has to back down every time an act of aggression is committed by a nuclear-armed power, it will be backing down more and more in the years to come. These are the kinds of questions we may have to get used to facing if the liberal world order continues to break down. For the past thirty years, would-be disrupters of the order have been deterred even from bringing things to such a point, but in a world where the United States appeared no longer determined to uphold the order, they may choose a different and more dangerous course.

China has been a more cautious player than Russia these past few years, but that may be changing. Chinese leaders were careful in part because, like Russia, they had been constrained by American power and the coherence of the liberal world order. But they were also cautious because, unlike Russia, they had thrived in the present order. In the American-led liberal order, Russia has fallen from superpower status, but China has risen toward it. Indeed, there are few countries in the world that have benefited more from the order, despite the fact that China has never been fully part of it. For the better part of two centuries, China was preyed upon by the English, the French, the Russians, the Germans, and then, most brutally, by the Japanese, who invaded and occupied swaths of China from 1915 onward. After the American victory over Japan in World War II, China was liberated from these foreign predators. Japan was defeated, the British and French empires were going out of business, and after the direct and indirect confrontations with the United States in Korea and Vietnam—both initiated by Mao—a rapprochement in the late 1960s offered protection against a hostile Soviet Union. The result, when Mao left the scene, was that China enjoyed an opportunity, unprecedented in its recent history, to take something of a holiday from geopolitics, to concentrate on internal development and become the economic dynamo it is today. With its security essentially safeguarded by the United States, with Chinese trade flowing freely on waterways kept open by the U.S. Navy, in a world of great-power peace preserved by American power and the liberal order, China could spend only a small percentage of its growing GDP on defense while pursuing Deng Xiaoping's foreign policy of "keeping a low profile and biding time."

China might have continued on this path for quite some time, growing rich and economically influential while the United States provided overall global and regional security and kept China's potential adversaries, like Japan, under control. That is certainly the course American officials in successive administrations had hoped China would take. But it is not the approach China has taken in recent years. As China has grown richer, more powerful, and more secure, Chinese leaders and the Chinese people have returned to old visions of hegemony. "China has been a great power" before and deserves to be one again, they insist. In recent years, ultranationalist books like *China Is Unhappy* have been national best sellers and reflect a growing segment of Chinese public opinion.[143] Even mainstream Chinese thinkers insist that China needs to be more assertive in its region and on the world stage. Strategic thinkers like Yan Xuetong argue that while "keeping a low profile" sufficed in Deng's time when China was relatively weak, now that China has become more powerful and risen to a new international stature, "continuing low-profile type policies will bring more harm than benefit."[144]

The "harm" they will bring does not have to do with security. The Chinese have no reason to fear attack from the United States, or even from Japan so long as the United States remains involved in the region. Nor do Chinese thinkers like Yan Xuetong even claim that China faces the threat of foreign invasion or attack. What the Chinese fear is they will be prevented from achieving their larger goals as a nation. According to Chinese scholar Wang Jisi, they see the United States trying to "prevent the emerging powers, in particular China, from achieving their goals and enhancing their stature." In the first instance this means the unification of Taiwan with the mainland and international recognition of Chinese control of the South China Sea. The Chinese have taken to calling these "core interests," thereby suggesting that the denial of these ambitions is itself a kind of attack on Chinese security. Nineteenth-century Americans made a similar claim with the Monroe Doctrine, which also asserted a hegemony they did not yet have the power to exercise, but they got away with it. The world was configured to their advantage. China's challenge is that the world is not configured to its advantage, at least not yet. They aim to change that. When Chinese thinkers and officials insist that "biding time" and "keeping a low profile" are no longer acceptable approaches, they mean they no longer find this situation tolerable. Again, this is not a security dilemma, for it is not primarily security that China seeks. It is the dilemma posed when a rising power sees its path blocked by existing power arrangements.

For some time the Chinese have debated whether to continue on Deng's cautious path or to embark on a new, more aggressive course. Today the more confrontational approach is ascendant. Some of this shift is due to changing perceptions of Chinese power relative to the United States. Some of it is generational. For Deng's generation, the achievements of the 1980s were a miracle after what China had experienced over the previous two centuries. Keeping a low profile and biding time was a way of not risking it all. The latest generation of Chinese rulers, however, is no longer content with past achievements. They have a new China dream. A similar transition occurred in Germany in the nineteenth century, when Bismarck's generation, which had been content with Germany's unification and its powerful, central position in Europe, gave way to a younger generation that was not content and sought equality with Great Britain on the world stage. China's leader, Xi Jinping, has made clear that China seeks equality with the United States, both as a leader and as a model for other nations. The "Chinese nation," he declared last year, "has stood up, grown rich, and is becoming strong." Therefore, China must now become "a global leader in terms of comprehensive national strength and international influence" as well as an alternative to the liberal democratic model, a "new option for other countries."[145]

China watchers used to argue that as the Chinese economy progressed, this would lead over time to the liberalization of Chinese domestic politics. This was necessary, they argued, if China was to continue climbing the ladder of production in an information age that presumably rewarded freer and more open societies. As President Clinton put it, "Without the full freedom to think, question, to create, China will be at a distinct disadvantage, competing with fully open societies in the information age where the greatest source of national wealth is what resides in the human mind."[146] Political and economic liberalization at home would, in turn, lead to more moderate and accommodating policies abroad as Chinese businesses sought deeper penetration in the liberal economic order. The result of these liberal assumptions was an American policy toward China that aimed to ease tensions, avoid provocation, and thereby allow moderate forces in China to steer a non-confrontational course.

This faith in theories of political and economic development, however, has proved misplaced.[147] China in recent years has achieved adequate growth without liberalization, and it has been increasingly assertive in the world without damaging its economy. Today, as Xi consolidates his power in a manner not seen since the days of Mao, Chinese foreign policy seems to be hardening further.

The big question for the Chinese is whether the United

States is willing to risk war to defend the order it created in East Asia or whether it is in retreat from the region it has dominated since 1945. If American commitments remain firm, the Chinese still face significant obstacles. Despite their growing power and influence, they have few allies and are surrounded by other great powers, most of which are allied with or have security agreements with the United States. If the United States is strong and determined and the liberal order remains healthy and united, a Chinese challenge could fail, which would pose domestic risks to the Chinese leadership. The Chinese recall Japan's ill-fated confrontation with the United States, when the Japanese won early victories and "ran wild" for a while, as Admiral Yamamoto predicted, but were eventually crushed by America's overwhelming industrial strength, its near invulnerability to attack, and its many allies—as Yamamoto also predicted. The Chinese must know that although they might also score early victories in a war with the United States, over Taiwan or in the South China Sea, they would wake the sleeping giant again, with all its industrial might and its global alliances, and over the long term they would lose.

But that assumes the sleeping giant can be awakened a second time. The danger will come if and when Chinese leaders perceive that the United States is too weak or is simply unwilling to continue upholding the liberal order in East Asia. Taking aggressive action would still be a gamble, but it is the kind of gamble rising powers are sometimes prone to take.

The problem today is not that geopolitics have returned, that Russia and China have begun to pursue old ambitions which had briefly been in abeyance. That was inevitable. The problem is that the liberal world order itself may no longer be healthy enough and coherent enough to continue containing and discouraging such ambitions as it has for the last seven decades. The will and capacity to resist these natural forces are declining in the United States and elsewhere. Nations and peoples within the order are themselves slipping back into old ruts, and in some respects the United States has been hastening the process.

One example is Japan, where old nationalist impulses long submerged and suppressed first by the American occupation and then by Japan's stunning economic growth have been reemerging. Some of this was probably inevitable. The generations that experienced World War II and Japan's crushing defeat have been gradually dying off—the current prime minister, Shinzo Abe, was born in 1954. New generations are naturally more inclined to ask why Japan cannot be a more "normal" nation again, which in their case means possessing a stronger, less constrained military and greater independence from Japan's American ally on matters of foreign policy. The long economic stagnation following the boom years of the 1970s and 1980s deprived the Japanese of the pride and honor they enjoyed as one of the world's most dynamic nations—a substitute for the pride in Japan's geopolitical standing in the prewar era.[148] New generations also suffer from what they call "apology fatigue." They are tired of incessant demands, particularly by China and South Korea, that Japan apologize for crimes committed before and during the Second World War. In China's case, they see these demands as attempts to weaken Japan's standing in the region. Many Japanese increasingly deny there is anything to apologize for.

Japanese history textbooks increasingly omit or minimize past misdeeds.[149] Abe has insisted that the Japanese must not let their "children, grandchildren and even further generations to come, who have nothing to do with that war, be predestined to apologize."[150] In Germany, far-right fringe groups express similar views, but no national leader would dare to do so. Nationalist narratives of the past that are forbidden in Germany are increasingly prevalent in Japan. Japanese nationalism is unmistakably on the rise, and in ways other powers in the region find worrying.

The United States in recent years has done more to encourage this rising nationalist sentiment than to quiet it. Despite American assurances to the contrary, the United States has come to be regarded as a less reliable guarantor of Japanese and regional security. Japan, unlike Germany, lives in a threatening environment, and the threats are growing. China is pursuing its more aggressive and contentious course, including against Japan in the East China Sea, and the danger from North Korea has been growing considerably. America's failure to address both these challenges adequately, at least from the Japanese perspective, has raised already prevalent doubts about America's staying power in the region. The Japanese, like the Chinese, perceive Americans to be in a declinist mood. They can see with their own eyes that U.S. naval forces are stretched thin, and that Congress still won't allocate sufficient resources to increase American capabilities substantially. They wonder, as do many Americans themselves, whether the United States is not, in fact, in a state of terminal decline. Their concerns began in the George W. Bush years, when the United States seemed distracted by wars in the Middle East, but ironically the event that may have had the biggest

effect on Japanese thinking was President Obama's decision not to use force in Syria in 2013. As one aide to Abe
put it afterward, if the United States no longer wants to be
"the world's policeman," then Japan can no longer "count
on America to protect us." Such concerns have only has-
tened Japan on its more nationalist course, with implications
for regional peace and even the possibility of conflict with
China.[151]

And what of America's allies in Europe? One month before
the British vote to leave the EU in the summer of 2016, then
British prime minister David Cameron asked, "Can we be
so sure that peace and stability on our continent are assured
beyond any shadow of doubt?" It would have been a remarkable question to ask even a decade earlier, when Europeans
still believed they were destined to "run the 21st century,"
but today the question is not quite as ridiculous as we'd like
to believe. As the British historian Niall Ferguson has commented, "history should discourage us from overestimating
the stability of the European continent."[152] The broad European peace established after the Cold War is less than three
decades old. The European Union is even younger. Prior to
World War II, the longest peace Europe enjoyed lasted forty-
three years, from the end of the Franco-Prussian War in
1871 to the outbreak of World War I in 1914, and the next
peace, such as it was, lasted just two decades. Those wars were
brought on by growing nationalism, global instability, and
the breakdown of the world order that had existed in the
nineteenth century. Those conditions are returning.

In all three of those nineteenth- and twentieth-century
wars, the main issue was Germany—a Germany that had
grown too rich, populous, and powerful for the other Euro-

pean powers to balance or contain, and a Germany that felt increasingly insecure surrounded by increasingly nervous and hostile neighbors. Today any thought of a conflict involving Germany seems incredible, given the liberal and pacific nature of the German people. Yet there is no denying that Europeans are watching more closely, as Cameron's comments showed. It was less than three decades ago, after all, that many Europeans viewed the prospect of a unified Germany with unease, the British and French in the West, the Poles and the Russians and others in the East.[153] French president François Mitterrand openly worried about setting the clock back to 1913. British Prime Minister Margaret Thatcher questioned whether a united Germany would not, "by its very nature," be a "destabilizing force" in Europe.[154] The British historian Michael Howard acknowledged that while the "German problem" might only be "a problem of perception," nevertheless it existed.[155] Germans themselves were acutely aware of the issue. The German thinker Ralf Dahrendorf found it "amazing how quickly the German bogey" had arisen in Europe, but even he had to admit in 1990 that, "when it comes to Germany, I am torn between hopes and fears, as I suppose many of us are all over Europe."[156]

The answer, at the time, was provided by the Americans. The administration of George H. W. Bush and Germany's Helmut Kohl hurried to offer reassurance by promising that all of Germany would be brought into NATO. Indeed, the "German question" was an unspoken reason why NATO survived the end of the Cold War—not to contain Russia, and not to go "out of area" to help the United States police the world, but simply to preserve the peace and stability of Europe itself. And ever since then, fears of the "German problem" have proved quite unfounded. Americans still complain about Germans' low military spending and their reluctance to use what military power they have. The rest of Europe, however, cannot be so unhappy that Germans remain among the most liberal and peace-loving people in the world, acutely conscious of their past and more wary than Japan of heading down the route of increasing nationalism and self-reliance.

But the "German problem" was never only about the character and choices of the Germans. It was also about geographical, demographic, economic, and geopolitical realities. Germany may have had a complicated path to "modernity," as many historians argue, but it has also had to navigate a complicated set of international circumstances, the most serious of which was a unified Germany that was too big for a Europe crowded with competitive great powers. It has only been within the multiple constraints of the liberal world order, including membership in both the EU and NATO, that Germany has managed to enjoy a tolerable level of mutual trust with its neighbors.

Germans themselves have played the most critical role in establishing this trust, by helping build the European Community and the European Union, and, crucially, by abandoning their cherished deutschmark for the euro and thus tying their economic fate to the rest of Europe, and also by working to strengthen NATO after reunification. As the German strategic thinker Christoph Bertram notes, when Germany unified, its leaders knew they had to "accommodate the concern of those worried about the German past as well as that of those troubled by its new power." Germany had to "use its weight and power wisely, considerately as well as confidently."[157] By and large, it did. Germany has been like a Gulliver who tied himself down on the beach and asked the Lilliputians to make sure he couldn't get up. But he could get up if he chose, and that's where the Americans have come in, an even bigger giant able to provide reassurance not only to the Lilliputians but to the Germans as well that the past was the past and that a unified Germany could safely prosper within a peaceful Europe.

But the past isn't just the past, not for Germany or any other great power, and some of the essential aspects of Germany's historical predicament remain. These days it is not Germany's military power but its economic power that causes fear and resentment in Europe, especially now that the German economy has been tied directly through the European monetary union to other economies that are less successful and less disciplined, including Italy, Greece, and Spain. More than one German statesman has warned his countrymen to beware of seeming to push other Europeans around. The former chancellor Helmut Schmidt, speaking to the Social Democratic Party's conference in 2011, warned, "If we Germans were to be tempted by our economic strength into claiming a leading political role in Europe, an increasing majority of our neighbors would mount effective resistance. This would cripple the EU and Germany would lapse into isolation."[158]

It is not impossible to imagine such a scenario, and the prospects increase as Europeans become more nationalistic, less cosmopolitan, more tribal, less "European." Which is precisely what is happening today in practically every European nation. If nationalism comes to dominate European politics again, how long before German nationalism returns, if only as a defense against suspicious and increasingly nationalistic neighbors? In 1945 Thomas Mann suggested that German behavior was a consequence of events, not character: "There are not two Germanys, a good one and a bad one," he argued, "but only one, whose best turned evil through devilish cunning. Wicked Germany is merely good Germany gone astray, good Germany in misfortune, in guilt and ruin."[159] The environment in which Germans live has an impact on how they act. Our abnormal era of peace and security has been the answer for seven decades; a return to normal would be worrying.

Yet there is no avoiding the fact that the European environment is deteriorating. On the economic front, the crises of Greece and Italy have been quieted for the moment, but the difficulties remain, as does the vast imbalance of economic power within Europe, which causes resentments in countries unhappy with German demands for fiscal austerity just as it causes resentments in Germany for having to subsidize the failing economies of nations they regard as irresponsible and profligate. The European Union was intended to quash nationalist tensions in Europe, but in this and other ways it may have exacerbated them. For the past few decades Germany has lived in a set of circumstances that made trust on all sides possible—a healthy German democracy in a healthy democratic Europe undergirded by a reliable American security guarantee. But what if Europe became less healthy and less democratic, more nationalistic and more fractured, less confident and less trusting? And what if at the same time the American security guarantee became less reliable? Would Germans be immune to such a radical change in their environs? If Europe returned to past patterns, could Germans avoid being dragged back with the rest?

We may find out, because unfortunately Europe is showing

signs of returning to past patterns. There has been a continent-wide populist rebellion against the European Union and the governments that abide by its rules, and against a cosmopolitan European elite that is allegedly out of touch with the concerns of the average Pole, Hungarian, Italian, Greek, German, or Briton. Some of those concerns are economic and stem from the global recession and the euro crisis. Much is a response to the floods of immigrants and refugees that have poured into Europe chiefly from the Middle East and North Africa and will be augmented, many fear, by another massive flow from sub-Saharan Africa. Democracy fares best when people feel relatively secure and poorly when they are or perceive themselves to be insecure. And security is about more than physical safety. When people feel their culture and way of life threatened, they look to their own for protection. It may or may not have been true that Middle Eastern or North African refugees were taking Europeans' jobs—the evidence suggests they were not. Nor did it matter whether acts of terror in Paris and London were carried out by new refugees or by second- or even third-generation immigrants. What mattered was that peoples across Europe perceived a risk to their livelihoods, to some extent to their security, but most of all to their culture. People throughout Europe feared their cultures would be swamped and disappear. Today, as a result, there is more reason to question the durability of the European project as it has unfolded since the end of the Second World War.

Some Americans, including President Trump, may not like the European Union any more than many Britons and continental Europeans do. Its flaws are apparent. Yet it is a symbol of Europe's determination not to return to its nationalist and bloody past. And it is more than a symbol. It binds European countries together in ways that annoy and cause conflict but also in ways that make European disintegration less likely. Those who suggest that Europe would be more harmonious without the EU have history against them. The EU is also the organization that, along with NATO, helps provide reassurance to Germany's neighbors and to Germans themselves. Those within the Eurozone who view Germany as a bullying behemoth should ask themselves whether they would have less concern if the EU disintegrated and Germany were no longer constrained by it. Would its economy be less dominant, its influence less potent? Nor is the issue only Germany's relations with its neighbors. The neighbors have their own issues, their own territorial and nationalist disputes stemming from the many ways Eastern and Central Europe in particular have been carved up over the centuries. Under the EU and within NATO, these disputes have been largely contained, but there is no reason to assume they would stay contained were pan-European institutions to collapse. As the political scientist Ivan Krastev has put it, Europe's "disintegration" will "transform a sympathetic environment of tolerance and openness to one characterized by a bullying narrow-mindedness."[160] It is hard to believe that a Europe without the European Union could remain peacefully postmodern.

This is especially true given the crisis of democracy that is spreading across Europe today, a crisis that is only partly related to the undemocratic aspects of the EU. This past year Europe dodged a bullet when Emmanuel Macron won the elections in France over populist nationalist Marine Le Pen, and when the Dutch populist Geert Wilders failed in the elections in Holland. The fact that there were widespread sighs of relief over those two outcomes, however, shows how far the right-wing nationalist parties have come in Europe. Elsewhere the gains of right-wing nationalist parties continue, as does the dismantling and undermining and general shakiness of democratic institutions in important nations like Hungary, Poland, the Czech Republic, and Slovakia. Nor can anyone be confident of the state of democracy in Italy (especially after the triumph of two populist parties with strong ties to Vladimir Putin). Italy was not a unified country with a common language before the late nineteenth century. The Italian republic was born after World War II. Italian democracy is young and, in some ways, untested because it has grown up only behind the shield of a healthy liberal world order. That is true of many European countries. Even with the order still intact, nationalist populism is on the rise, and if it continues, we can expect "more authoritarian law-and-order policies," "more polarized political debates," "more demagogic leaders," greater opposition to the EU and NATO, and "greater sympathy for Russia," as *The Economist* notes.[161] After decades of democratic progress in Europe, Krastev observes, "the democracy question" is today "at the heart of Europe's troubles."[162]

It would not be the first time. After the First World War, the number of democracies in the world had doubled, and most of these were in Europe. But with Britain and France reeling from the war, and the United States retreating from the continent, many of these new democracies began to fall and fascism began to rise. Of the twenty-six parliamentary democracies in place in 1919, only twelve were still around two decades later. There was no single dramatic event that signaled the shift. As Hannah Arendt pointed out, revolutionary change came without revolutionary upheaval. In Italy the government fell to "a few thousand almost unarmed people" who staged a march on Rome led by a journalist and former socialist named Benito Mussolini, who was part revolutionary, part nationalist reactionary, and part opportunistic demagogue. In Poland, a motley coalition of nobles and peasants, workers and employers, Catholics and Orthodox Jews all supporting "semi-fascist government" won two-thirds of the seats in Parliament.[163] In Portugal, Spain, Hungary, the Baltic states, and Romania, as well as in Italy, Germany, and Poland, mostly right-wing movements captured control of governments peacefully and then put an end to democratic forms.[164] None of this had much to do with Hitler and Mussolini. As the historian Ira Katznelson points out, liberalism as an idea simply failed. Many came to regard democratic institutions as illegitimate, "sham protectors of plutocracy and bourgeois domination against the collective interests of the people and the nation."[165] Meanwhile, the great-power democracies were weak, divided, and inward-looking. The liberal order had broken down and been replaced by a competitive multipolar struggle in which raw power mattered more than ideas and institutions. Amidst such uncertainty and insecurity, people increasingly looked to their tribe, their race, and their nation for protection. The fascist governments looked stronger, more energetic and efficient, than the democracies, and they appealed directly and effectively to nationalist, ethnic, and tribal fears.

All this should sound familiar. Today's Europe may be a far cry from the Europe of the 1930s. The problem is, we don't know how far. New forms of insecurity are driving people back to tribalism. Liberalism seems to provide no answers, and indeed in the eyes of many it is precisely the liberal Enlightenment ideals of freedom and cosmopolitanism that are to blame. As Krastev observes, "The immediate post-1989 excitement prompted by the shattering of walls has been replaced by a dizzying anxiety and a demand to build fences."[166]

For the first time since World War II, a far-right nationalist party has risen to claim a significant position in German politics. The Alternative für Deutschland gained ninety-two seats in parliamentary elections last year, making it the third largest party in the Bundestag. Ninety-five percent of AfD voters said they feared a "loss of German culture and language" as a result of the influx of immigrants and refugees from the Middle East. But the newly popular party stands for more than opposition to immigration. Like some Japanese nationalists, many Germans who support such populist nationalist parties are tired of apologizing for Germany's past sins, tired of what they call the *Schuldkult,* or "cult of guilt," and tired of all the remembrances of the Holocaust, which they either deny or minimize. As the scholar Timothy Garton Ash has observed, German politics are moving right, and it "is a new German right with distinct echoes of the old." A year ago, one AfD leader, complaining about the inundation of "culturally alien peoples," attributed it to the "pigs" in the German leadership who were "nothing other than puppets of the victor powers of the Second World War."[167] It doesn't really matter what spurs such thoughts. The rise of such nationalist sentiments has geopolitical implications, which is why liberal Germans worry today about the direction of their country, as do other Europeans. Americans need to be concerned, too.

. . .

The United States must accept its share of the blame for what has happened to Europe. President Obama's refusal to use adequate American force to restore some semblance of stability in Syria after the uprising against Bashar al-Assad in 2011 may have been understandable. There were, and are, no obvious or simple solutions to the Syrian crisis, and he was not wrong to worry that even a small intervention could put the United States on a slippery slope toward deeper involvement. In the 1990s a Bush or a Clinton might have intervened nevertheless—there had been no obvious simple solutions in Bosnia or Kosovo either—but Obama did not believe American power offered any answer or that the American people would approve it even if it did. As he acknowledged, "It's not that it's not worth it. It's that after a decade of war, you know, the United States has limits."[168]

Here was the "restraint" that critics of American foreign policy had been calling for, yet the price of restraint has proved high, and not only in the Middle East but in Europe. Poll data show that the inpouring of millions of refugees from Syria (and to a lesser extent from Libya) contributed more than any other factor to the rising popularity of nationalist, ultranationalist, and even overtly fascist political parties across Europe. The European refugee crisis brought on by the Syrian crisis has rattled democratic institutions right in the heart of the liberal world order.[169] As international relations scholar Thomas Wright has noted, Obama and his advisers believed Europe could take care of itself and should be left to do so. Europe's "travails were its own fault and responsibility," and although the United States could help, Europe fundamentally had to solve its own problems. This may have seemed perfectly rational to Americans—it was what the "realist" Robert A.

Taft had argued in the 1930s—but it was, as Wright notes, "a significant shift."[170] The United States had not left Europe to solve its own problems after 1945 or during the Cold War, or even after the Cold War. The Atlantic Community was where the liberal world order began, and it has remained the heart of that order. For the United States to suggest that Europe needed less attention raised doubts not only in Europe but around the world about America's commitment to the order. Obama's famous "pivot" to Asia has, for this reason, as well as because of the evident lack of resources committed to it, done nothing to reassure Asian allies, either.

Doubts about America have reverberated across the globe, especially since the election of Trump, and this alone has contributed to the unraveling of the liberal order. Perceptions of global and geopolitical trends have a greater effect on the decisions of leaders and the behavior of people around the world than we imagine. When fascism was on the rise in Europe in the 1920s and 1930s, people were more inclined to fascism, even in Latin America and Africa. When communism seemed on the rise in the 1950s and 1960s, others were more inclined to carry that banner on the other side of the world. When the democracies emerged as the most successful powers after 1989, people wanted to join that winning team. It's no surprise then that the widespread conviction, following the economic crisis of 2008, that the United States was in decline—a conviction encouraged by Americans themselves—has had an impact around the world, including in Europe. When Hungarian president Viktor Orbán spoke out to celebrate the "illiberal state" a few years ago, he claimed he was only responding to new global realities: "the great redistribution of global financial, economic, commercial, political and military power that became obvious in 2008."[171] The idea that the "post-American world" had begun, that, as the German finance minister put it, the United States would "lose it superpower status in the global financial system," has had its effect on the direction of peoples and their leaders.[172]

In fact, the latest predictions of American decline are proving as mistaken as all previous such predictions. The American economy has strengthened. America's share of global GDP, which dipped slightly after the recession of 2008, has bounced back. The common assumption that the United States cannot possibly sustain its position in East Asia in the face of a rising China overestimates Chinese strength and underestimates America's persistent strategic advantages. Not least of these is its continuing close alliances with the region's other great powers. It is no more accurate to say today that the West is facing inevitable decline than it was to say in 1989 that history had ended and liberalism had triumphed.

The bigger questions concern Americans' commitment to the liberal world order. That commitment has rested on two pillars. One was the reliable security guarantee that the United States provided, which kept the world from returning to its pre-1945 historical patterns and which sustained the general peace and the prosperity and democratic progress that flowed from it. The other pillar was the liberal compact that bound the United States and the other members of the order together. In exchange for nations forgoing traditional geopolitical ambitions and ceding the United States a near monopoly of military power, the United States would support an open economic order in which others would be allowed to compete and succeed; it would not treat members of the order, and particularly allies, simply as competitors in a zero-sum game;

and it would through participation in international institutions, an active multilateral diplomacy, and the articulation of shared liberal values support and sustain a sense of community among those nations that made common cause on behalf of those shared values and interests. The United States was not always faithful to this compact, and nor were other members of the order always faithful to it. But its leaders never denied or rejected America's responsibilities and generally attempted to live up to them.

In recent years, however, it has become increasingly apparent that Americans no longer feel bound to carry out those responsibilities and have even begun to regard them as contrary to their interests. There were glimmers of this during the Obama administration, when senior officials went out of their way to denigrate the bipartisan foreign policy consensus that stood for this traditional American approach. Obama himself complained about allies acting as "free-riders." In calling for "nation building here at home," he was suggesting that an active American foreign policy detracted from Americans' domestic well-being. During Obama's two terms, allies around the world came to doubt the reliability of the American security guarantee more than in the past, and Russia and China, each in their own way, worked increasingly effectively to chip away at the liberal order.

With the election of Trump, the other shoe has fallen. As a candidate, Trump and his supporters went much further than Obama. They did not just call for retrenchment in American foreign policy. They criticized and repudiated the liberal world order. Trump explicitly rejected America's responsibility to carry out its part of the liberal compact. He wanted "victories" on trade deals, and not just over China but over close allies like Canada and Germany. Allies were now competitors. Against them, too, the United States had to "win." In the past the goal had not been to beat other nations, and least of all allies, but to seek mutual advantage in the interests of a free trade regime that bolstered peaceful relations among economic competitors. Trump's approach meant a different kind of system entirely, a struggle of all against all. As two of Trump's top advisers explained "America First" early in his presidency, the world was not a "global community." It was "an arena where nations . . . engage and compete for advantage." The United States brings to this competition "unmatched military, political, economic, cultural and moral strength." This, they argued, was an "elemental nature of international affairs."[173] But that was not how the United States had viewed the liberal world order in the past. A central premise of postwar foreign policy was that the United States would *not* bring its "unmatched" strength to bear in a competition with its allies and other members of the liberal world order. As the international relations scholar Daniel W. Drezner has pointed out, for the most powerful country in the world to embrace such a Hobbesian vision even when dealing with its own allies would be to invite a Hobbesian response by everyone else.[174] If the core compact of the liberal world order is broken, how long before the other members of the order begin to view the United States as no longer deserving of their trust and cooperation?

If Obama's policies put a dent in the liberal world order, Trump's statements and actions are driving a stake through it. For if the United States cannot be relied upon to provide the secure environment in which members of the liberal world order can flourish, and if it is going to be jealous and spiteful and demand "wins" when they do flourish, then the United States starts to look more like a rogue superpower than a nation defending any order of any kind. To the degree that this impression takes hold, it will sap the liberal order of what remains of its confidence and cohesion, and just at the moment that Russia and China are contemplating how far to go in challenging it.

THE AMERICAN JUNGLE

Of course it is hard to support a liberal order when liberalism is under attack at home. Lurking behind much of the criticism of American foreign policy on both left and right is dissatisfaction with America itself. Debates about foreign policy have often been proxies for debates about the nation's meaning and identity, from the conflict between Hamilton and Jefferson over the young republic's relationships with England and Revolutionary France to the Vietnam-era debates over the rights and wrongs of democratic capitalism. Today again the criticisms of America's decades-long support for a liberal international order are as much reflections of domestic battles over the nation's identity as they are about foreign policy. Belief that America's democratic capitalist system is failing in some fundamental way at home, a belief shared across the political spectrum, has contributed to the collapse of support for an American foreign policy designed to uphold a liberal democratic capitalist order.

During the Cold War, this critique came almost exclusively from the left, and modern "progressives" continue that assault today. The Democratic Party has increasingly become the party of "progressives." Unlike the liberals of the past, who sought to compensate for liberal capitalism's failings but believed, in the words of historian Sean Wilentz, that it was "a proven engine of innovation, opportunity, and mass prosperity," many of the new progressives revile capitalism and yearn for socialism. Not the Soviet type, of course. They somehow believe that Sweden is a "socialist" country, not realizing that, as Wilentz points out, Sweden is a capitalist country, a social democracy with a welfare state. (As Ralf Dahrendorf once quipped, "Sweden" is not Sweden; "it is a dream with no base anywhere on the map of Europe.") And while liberals believed that American power had been "used for good beyond our borders," without ignoring the bad it had also done, progressives "assume that the exercise of American power abroad, especially military power, is almost always malevolent." They see "no significant distinction between interventionism and imperialism." They oppose not only the exercise of American power but the liberal world order itself, which many progressives view as nothing more than American hegemony on behalf of rich white men.[175]

This critique of America and its foreign policy has long been a staple of the left, but in recent years it has also become a prominent feature of conservative thought. Traditional American conservatism was always hostile to an activist foreign policy, which conservatives correctly saw as strengthening the powers of the federal government and of the executive branch. In the first half of the twentieth century, "progressives" like Wilson and the two Roosevelts spoke of America's "international responsibilities," while conservatives championed "normalcy." The Cold War was an aberration, when conservatives favored global opposition to communism, but when the Soviet Union fell, many conservatives returned to their traditional posture. Patrick Buchanan's 1999 book, *A Republic, Not an Empire,* echoed the anti-federalists' critique of the Constitution in 1787 as a blueprint for a "great and mighty empire" that would destroy American liberties.[176]

Conservative hostility to internationalism and the liberal world order is also rooted in a conservative critique of the Enlightenment principles that helped inspire the American Revolution and which were embodied in the Declaration of Independence. Some conservative intellectuals have preferred to locate America's democratic virtues in the country's early Anglo-Saxon Protestant political and cultural heritage, rather than in the universal principles of the Enlightenment. This perspective has sometimes taken the form of a kind of ethno-nationalism, in which the waves of non-Protestant, non-Anglo-Saxon, and nonwhite immigrants are seen as diluting the culture and traditions on which American democracy was supposedly founded. Since debates about American foreign policy are always partly debates about American identity, there has invariably been a foreign policy component to this concern.

The 1920s combined rising white nationalism, restrictive immigration policies designed to shut off all immigration except from Northern Europe (such that Hitler feared the United States, not Germany, would become the true Aryan nation), with a foreign policy that explicitly repudiated internationalism as anti-American. Many in the America First movement in 1940 took a sympathetic view of German arguments. Charles Lindbergh was not alone in believing that a "Europe dominated by Germany" would "maintain the supremacy of our western civilization."[177] Those views were suppressed during a war fought explicitly against Nazism and its racial theories, and the Cold War competition brought some effort to square America's principles with its practices. But when the Cold War ended, some Americans returned to earlier concerns about the nation's social and cultural identity. Samuel Huntington, in his later years, expressed alarm that America's Anglo-Protestant "identity" was being swamped by "multiculturalism," and he both predicted and even cautiously endorsed a new "white nativism" in response to the attack on whites' "culture" and "power" by the expanding influence of Hispanics.[178] His post–Cold War writings about a "clash of civilizations" urged Americans to pull back from the world and tend to their own "Western" civilization.

Such views permeate conservative and Republican foreign policy thinking today. Not only do conservatives, and many other Americans, regard Islam as incompatible with democracy (much as many once regarded Catholicism as incompatible with democracy). Some decry the very idea of liberal universalism as a "false ideology . . . a cancer on our body politic." They not only criticize American support for democracy in supposedly "unfit" cultures overseas but also warn that the "import en masse" of "people from other cultures" lacking Judeo-Christian traditions poses a threat to democracy at home.[179] Such views are widespread among the nationalist populist movements in Europe, and both Trump and his one-time top adviser, Steve Bannon, have consistently supported and made common cause with those abroad who share this anxiety for the preservation of white Christian culture against dark-skinned, non-Christian immigrants.

These attacks on the Enlightenment universalism on which the country was founded should not be dismissed as

cranky aberrations. The United States also has its "subterranean stream" running through its history, from the slavehold-
ing South to the Know-Nothings to the white supremacists of
the Jim Crow era and the revival of the Klan of the 1920s to
the alt-right of today. Although we prefer to forget or down-
play the whole boiling cauldron of angers and hatreds and
resentments which have been such a big part of our history,
the jungle grows in America, too.

Americans may well come out of it, at least partly, as they
have in the past. Their politicians can run roughshod over
institutions and even over the Constitution, but Americans
cannot escape the principles of the Declaration, even if they
want to. They have nowhere else to go. Other nations can fall
back on blood-and-soil nationalism, but Americans have no
such nationalism to fall back on, regardless of what Trump
and his white nationalist supporters might wish. Huntington and others miss a critical point about the founding of
the American republic. The authors of the Declaration of
Independence were indeed Anglo-Protestants, most of whom
did not believe that Catholics were fit for democracy (nor
were women, much less blacks or Asians or Muslims). However, they consciously and explicitly rejected the idea that the
rights they claimed derived from their status as English-
men, nor did they claim that only Anglo-Protestants could
be trusted to protect and advance those rights. They even
recognized that the slavery they wrote into the Constitution
contradicted their universalist claims and anticipated the day
when slavery would wither and the contradiction would be
resolved. The universal principles they enshrined in the Declaration had more lasting power than the Anglo-Protestant
culture from which they sprang. These continued to be the

driving force in American life—the "apple of gold," as Lincoln put it—superseding even the Constitution, ultimately leading to the abolition of slavery, the promise of rights for former slaves and for every group that followed, regardless of religion or cultural background. The continual expansion of rights to protected minorities is the one constant in American history. That is the essence of America as it was established by the founders, and though Americans often stray from it, eventually they are tugged back.

For as long as the latest eruption of Americans' subterranean stream lasts, however, it will be hard for the United States to pull out of its current trajectory and begin the climb back to international responsibility. To sustain a foreign policy of enlightened self-interest requires enlightenment, a degree of generosity, a belief in the universalism of rights, and, yes, a measure of cosmopolitanism that Americans have not lately been displaying. The danger is that by the time they come out of their current mood, it may be too late to repair the damage and stem the forces of nature and history.

PROTECTING THE GARDEN

A character in Hemingway's *The Sun Also Rises,* asked how he went bankrupt, responds, "Gradually and then suddenly." That is a fair description of how the world order collapsed before the two world wars, and of how it likely will collapse in our own time. Unfortunately, Americans have since forgotten how quickly it can happen, how graver threats than we anticipate can emerge to catch us physically and psychologically unprepared. One would think it hard to have a 1930s mentality knowing what happened in the 1940s, but we continually comfort ourselves that the horrors of seventy-five years ago cannot be repeated. We see no Hitlers or Stalins on the horizon, no Nazi Germany, no Imperial Japan, no Soviet Union. We believe that the leaders of today's potential adversaries, the Vladimir Putins and Xi Jinpings, are just run-of-the-mill authoritarians who only want a little respect and their own fair share of the international pie. They may be in it for the money or the glory, but they do not pose an existential threat to our way of life. We forget, of course, that people in the 1930s felt the same way about Hitler and Stalin.

Ivan Krastev jokes that "the question is no longer whether it's possible for Hitler to come back; it's whether we'd even be able to recognize him."[180] But it is not a joke: we almost certainly will not recognize the Hitlers and Stalins in our midst until they have emerged as full-blown, unmanageable threats. There are always dangerous people out there, lacking only the power and the opportunity to achieve their destiny. We used to take the ever-present evil in man more seriously. In 1973 the German social psychologist Erich Fromm wrote about man's inherent inclinations to "destructiveness" and "cruelty," the "specifically human" craving for "absolute control," the tendency to "malignant aggression." Even "the most sadistic and destructive man is human," he argued. "He can be called a warped and sick man who has failed to achieve a better answer to the challenge of having been born human, and this is true; he can also be called a man who took the wrong way in search of his salvation."[181] Many people have evil in them, and many of those people harbor grand designs, mad or not, that they never have a chance even to try to fulfill. They are constrained by the powers and forces around them, the "order," whatever it may be, and so they never have a chance to reveal their true selves, even to themselves. The circumstances in which Hitler, Stalin, and Mussolini rose to power—a world in which no nation was willing or able to sustain any kind of international order—gave them ample opportunity to show what they were capable of. Had there been an order in place to blunt those ambitions, we might never have come to know them as tyrants, aggressors, and mass killers. Perhaps if Weimar democracy had somehow survived, or if the Versailles Treaty had been effectively enforced, perhaps if the United States had done in 1919 what it later did in 1945, we might never have known the Hitler of our history books.

Today we know a Putin who has grand ambitions but not yet the capacity to realize them. He reveres Stalin but he is not Stalin. But what would a less constrained Putin be? What would a Russia that had restored its Soviet and imperial borders be? Today a more powerful China is departing from the cautious foreign policies of Deng's weaker China. What will an even more powerful and less constrained China be like? What would North Korea be if U.S. troops were withdrawn from the Korean Peninsula as part of some peace agreement? Who can say whether such powers might in time become a threat on a par with those we faced in the past if they are allowed to expand their regional and global influence by military means? The transition from Deng to Xi Jinping contradicts our beliefs about "modernization" and the "common evolutionary pattern" that Fukuyama celebrated. We wanted to believe that history was taking us away from the wars, tyranny, and destruction of the first half of the twentieth century, but history and human nature may be taking us back toward them, absent some monumental effort on our part to prevent such regression.

We have taken too much solace from the fact that our opponents are not communists but are merely authoritarians. During the Cold War, people like Jeane Kirkpatrick argued that Americans had nothing to fear from authoritarianism. Authoritarian governments would eventually evolve into democracies if given enough time, but "totalitarian" communism was forever. Of course this turned out not to be true at all. Communist governments in the Soviet Union and Eastern and Central Europe did fall, and not because they were toppled by American-backed rebels or opposition movements. In the Soviet Union and elsewhere, governments attempted to carry out peaceful reforms and to open the system, which ultimately led to the establishment of democracies, briefly in Russia and longer-lasting in Eastern and Central Europe. The right-wing dictatorships that fell after the Cold War, on the other hand—Suharto in Indonesia, Mubarak in Egypt—did not reform. In fact, they resisted reform until the very end, clamped down rather than eased repression, killed and jailed thousands of opposition leaders and protesters—something Gorbachev and most of the Eastern and Central European communist governments refused to do. Most of the authoritarian regimes that fell did so in large part because the United States withdrew support. Nor have the authoritarian regimes that survived or taken power since the Cold War, in Venezuela or the Arab world, shown any inclination to open or liberalize their systems. In China, the government has taken some of the trappings of communism and replaced them with an authoritarianism and one-man rule that may prove more durable. Authoritarianism these days has shown itself less susceptible to internal pressures for reform than communism did at the end, and more capable of withstanding the liberal pressures from outside.

One reason may be that communism sprang from the same Enlightenment roots as liberalism. In many ways it competed on the same plane, and it proved unable to compete. Because communism proposed such an extreme version of the Enlightenment, it conflicted even more with human nature than liberalism and so, on the one hand, had to impose its system with greater brutality, and, on the other hand, was even more likely to fall short of its own promises. It offered much that was appealing to the human soul—the promise of justice and true equality, an end to materialism—but it also demanded more than humans could give and ensured a far greater gap between dream and reality. When it failed to deliver, it suffered a crisis of confidence. When it was also deprived of geopolitical successes and fell behind in the Cold War competition for power and influence, even Soviet leaders had a hard time reconciling the promise of their ideology and the reality of its failure, just as Kennan had predicted.

Authoritarians don't have the same vulnerability. The case for authoritarianism during the Cold War was that it was traditional, organic, natural, yet perhaps the very naturalness of authoritarianism makes it a bigger and more enduring threat. We have assumed that authoritarianism is a stage in an evolutionary process. But there may be no stages. Authoritarianism may be a stable condition of human existence, more stable than liberalism and democracy. It appeals to core elements of human nature that liberalism does not always satisfy—the desire for order, for strong leadership, and perhaps above all, the yearning for the security of family, tribe, and nation. If the liberal world order stands for individual rights, freedom, universality, equality, regardless of race or national origin, for cosmopolitanism and tolerance, the authoritarian regimes of today stand for the opposite, and in a very traditional and time-honored way. After all, it was liberalism that was the newcomer which promised to overturn centuries of tradition. And it was greeted with hostility by those unpersuaded by its preachings. From the beginning, liberalism inspired a virulent anti-liberalism. Eighteenth- and nineteenth-century critics, sometimes referred to as leaders of a Counter-Enlightenment, took aim in particular at the universalism of the liberal world-view, the elevation of the individual and individual's rights above nation, tribe, and family. Such cosmopolitanism, they argued, uprooted tradition and culture and "all that makes one most human." They believed, as most people had always believed, in a natural "hierarchy of authority," preferring the "awe-inspiring power" of a Louis XIV to the chaos and impotence of liberalism. Humans were "not made for freedom"; it was only under "wisely authoritarian governments" that they could find happiness.[182]

Such anti-liberal views sprout up like natural antibodies wherever liberalism takes hold. They informed the German struggle on behalf of *Kultur* and the primacy of the state over the individual in World War I; they informed the fascist movements in the interwar years; in Asia, they inspired a defense of what used to be called "Asian values," which emphasize community over the individual, harmony over freedom. The present Chinese government's critique of liberalism is not so much a communist critique as a conservative critique. It could have been lifted from disgruntled remnants of the old German aristocracy during the Weimar era. In commenting on the "crises and chaos swamp[ing] Western liberal democracy" last year, the state-run news agency, Xinhua, noted that while in China communist and noncommunist parties worked together to preserve "social harmony" and "efficient policy making and implementation," in the liberal world "competitive, confrontational Western politics," the "endless political backbiting, bickering and policy reversals" had "retarded economic and social progress and ignored the interests of most citizens." After "several hundred years, the Western model" was "showing its age," and it was "high time for profound reflection on the ills of a doddering democracy which has precipitated so many of the world's ills and solved so few."[183] Putin and his political counselors have made much the same argument. Radical Islam is nothing if not a rejection of Enlightenment thinking in favor of spirituality and rigid adherence to religious tradition. The Counter-Enlightenment critique of liberalism will always appeal to those who see their traditional values and religious beliefs challenged and undermined by what they view as the cold materialism of the modern liberal world. It was not just globalization that caused the backlash among such peoples; it was the globalization of liberalism.

While we were grateful when communism collapsed, the liberal world order flourished when communism was the enemy. It is doing less well against a Counter-Enlightenment that plays more effectively on liberalism's failings and inse-curities. It is worth recalling that the most potent challenges to democracy in the first decades of the twentieth century came from the right, not the left. As the British historian Eric Hobsbawm once observed, "in the twenty years of lib-eral retreat" between the wars, "not a single regime that could be reasonably called liberal-democratic had been overthrown from the left. The danger came exclusively from the right. And the right represented not merely a threat to constitutional and representative government, but an ideological threat to liberal civilization as such, and a potentially worldwide movement, for which the label 'fascism' is both insufficient and not wholly relevant."[184] Gorbachev had more in common with liberals in the West than he did with many of his own people. Putin, with his stand against gay rights, his condemnation of the "genderless and infertile" morality of the liberal West, his support for the Russian Orthodox Church and for conservative traditions in general, may well speak for the majority of Russians in a way that Gorbachev did not.

And not just for Russians. Putin's message resonates in a Western Europe where disenchantment with liberalism, and the immigration it permits, is rising. It even resonates in the United States. Not so long ago, Patrick Buchanan called Putin the voice of "conservatives, traditionalists and nationalists of all continents and countries" who were standing up against "the cultural and ideological imperialism of . . . a decadent West."[185] And Buchananism is not the outlier it once was in American politics; in many ways it was Trumpism before Trump. These days, if the polls are to be believed, favorable views of Russia's "strong leader" have grown, at least among Trump's supporters. Putin has positioned himself as the leader of the world's "socially and culturally conservative" common folk against "international liberal democracy," and there probably are more of those common folk around the world, including in the West, than there ever were committed communists.[186] That is why Russian penetration of the political systems of the United States and Europe has been so effective. It has exploited the truly dangerous fissures in Western society, which are not based on class, as the Marxists wanted to believe, but on tribe and culture.

If so, the challenge to democracy today is greater than it

was during the Cold War when, after all, democracy quite successfully spread across the globe. We need to abandon the post–Cold War myth that liberalism must be the natural end point of human evolution because it triumphed over communism. Five thousand years of recorded history suggest that it isn't. And this is not because dictators prevent their people from choosing liberalism and self-government, which they would if only given a chance. Our belief that peoples at all times share a desire for freedom, and that this universal desire supersedes all others, is an incomplete description of human experience. People also seek order and security and may welcome a strong leader who can provide those things, even if he does not allow them the full panoply of rights and freedoms. In troubled times, and not only in troubled times, people seek outlets for anger and resentment, for fear and hatred of the "other" in their midst. Those who have suffered defeat and humiliation, such as Germans after World War I or Russians after the Cold War, often find that democracy offers insufficient solace and insufficient promise of revenge and justice, and they look to a strong leader to provide those things, too. They tire of the incessant arguing over national budgets and other trifles while the larger needs of the nation, including the spiritual and emotional needs, go unaddressed. We would like to believe that, at the end of the day, the desire for freedom trumps these other human impulses. But there is no end of the day, and there are no final triumphs. Human existence is a constant battle among competing impulses—between self-love and the love of others, between the noble and the base, between the desire for freedom and the desire for order and security—and because those struggles never end, the fate of liberalism and democracy in the world is never settled. It is an illusion to believe that the present democratic age is eternal rather than transient, or that it can survive without constant tending and constant defense.

It is also an illusion to believe that democracy is doomed or that it is not for us to help it survive where survival is difficult. These days critics of American foreign policy argue that the United States should not be trying to spread or support democracy where the natural conditions for it are supposedly lacking. What they generally mean is that we should not be trying to support democracy in the Islamic world. They don't mean Poland, or Hungary, or Italy. But are we so confident that democracy has a natural home even in the West, that Western Civilization with its supposedly Judeo-Christian values must always be a safe zone for democracy? History suggests otherwise. It was in the Christian West that fascism and communism arose; it was in avowedly Christian nations with Christian monarchs and established churches that the modern police state took root in the nineteenth century. It was in the Christian West that democracy collapsed after World War I. And it is in the Christian West that democracy is at risk today. Those who most vigorously proclaim their Christian values these days are the nationalist, populist, and quasi-fascist parties, and would-be authoritarian governments in Europe. Trump gave his speech lauding Western Civilization in Poland, yet it is by no means clear that Polish democracy will survive, despite its Christian heritage. If the United States actually supported democracy only where long traditions of liberalism and liberal institutions existed, we might find ourselves supporting only the half dozen or so that existed at the end of the nineteenth century.

Living in the bubble of the liberal world order these past

seven decades, we have lost sight of the fact that sustaining democracy is a constant struggle everywhere, both in the West and outside it. Liberal democracies have not been common in history. If they are not contrary to human nature, they are also not favored by it. Liberal democracy has survived and flourished in our time because the leading powers provide a zone of security within which it can be protected and allowed to overcome the natural obstacles to its success. They have tipped the scales in the ongoing struggle between democratic and nondemocratic forces that exist in every society, and they have done so in European and Asian nations where democracy had never taken hold and where less than a century ago it would have been unimaginable. Those who today believe that democracy is impossible in the Islamic world should recall that not so long ago people believed with equal conviction that democracy was impossible in Catholic and Asian countries. The United States and its partners poured hundreds of billions of dollars and millions of troops over several decades into growing and sustaining democracy in Europe and Asia. One wonders what the Islamic world would look like if a fraction of that time, effort, and resources had been devoted to nurturing democratic government there rather than to supporting a succession of dictatorships.

Despite everything that has happened, if we reject the counsels of the new "realism" and resume our support for the liberal world order, it is still within our capacity to defend it and put off its collapse, perhaps for quite some time. Today the order remains intact, despite the hostility of the present administration and the weakness of the last. The international structures supporting it are durable. This is partly because they rest on geographical realities and a distribution of power that still favor the liberal order and still pose obstacles to those who would disrupt it. It is also because liberal values, though under assault, remain a force that binds the democratic nations of the world together. Authoritarianism also has its appeal and will always compete with liberalism, but the authoritarian governments do not feel the same sense of commonality as the monarchies and aristocracies of the early nineteenth century. The Chinese and Russians are not adversaries, but they are not allies either. They share little except their antipathy to liberalism. The democratic nations, however, are bound together by more than common adversaries, as the post–Cold War era has proved. America's alliances in Europe and Asia have so far held, therefore, despite the weakening of America's commitment under two administrations. There is still a liberal world order to be salvaged, if the American people decide it is worth salvaging.

They will also have to decide that they are prepared to pay the costs, and those costs have not changed. It took great and consistent exertions of American power and influence to create and sustain this world order. It will take no less to continue upholding it into the future. Americans over the past two decades have become convinced that the United States is doing too much when actually it has been doing too little.

Much of what needs to be done to shore up the order requires only diplomatic and economic measures. The United States needs to return to the deep engagement with Europe that characterized the relationship from the postwar years to the early post–Cold War years. Americans must understand that a healthy liberal Europe is the anchor of the order from which they benefit. Therefore such matters as the negotiation of Britain's withdrawal from the EU, the Eurozone crisis, the cyber threats from Russia, and European energy supplies must be addressed not just as European problems but as transatlantic problems that affect the United States, too. The United States also needs to work with European governments to address the democratic backsliding in Europe. Nations that entered the EU and NATO after the Cold War had to meet high standards of democratic governance in order to gain membership. If some have ceased to meet those standards, they need to be suspended from membership or denied some of the benefits of membership. Hungary and Turkey cannot expect to enjoy the benefits of NATO, and, in Hungary's case, EU membership, so long as they celebrate their "illiberalism" and reject the basic premises of the liberal world order. Finally, the United States needs to return to the liberal compact when it comes to trade and international institutions. It was a serious blow to the liberal order when the United States walked away from the Trans-Pacific Partnership—and a great boon to China. The order will suffer further if American trade policies seek "wins" over close allies like Canada and Germany. Americans need to understand that the free trade regime undergirds the order from which they benefit as much or more than anyone. It is not a "win" if that regime collapses into the protectionism that characterized the decades before World War II.

Then there is the question of maintaining America's military predominance in the international system. For all the talk of "soft" power and "smart" power, it is ultimately the American security guarantee, the ability to deploy hard power to deter and defeat potential aggressors, that provides the essential foundation without which the liberal world order could never survive. Members of Congress from both parties have underfunded the military since the beginning of the post– Cold War era, but especially over the last decade. Defense secretaries from both parties have raised alarms about the increasing inability of the armed forces to perform their missions of deterrence around the world. And the dangers of war have only grown in recent years, not diminished. Americans need to remember that deterring a war is much less expensive than fighting one.

It is not only the money to preserve power, however, but also the willingness to apply that power, with all the pain and the suffering, the uncertainties and the errors, the failures and follies, the immorality and brutality, the lost lives and the lost treasure. Most of what we need to do to sustain the liberal order will not require sending troops, but there will be times when it will be necessary. It is simply dishonest to tell the American people that the relative security and prosperity they have enjoyed can be sustained without the occasional threat or use of force. There will be challenges on the Korean Peninsula, in the South China Sea, in the Middle East, and along the fault lines between Russia and NATO.

We would like to be sure that there will be no more Iraqs and Vietnams, and we should do our best, learning from past mistakes, to avoid such failures. But it would be foolish to imagine we can avoid mistakes and failures entirely. There is no doctrine other than pure isolation and inaction that can prevent such tragedies. The Obama administration offered a doctrine of not doing "stupid" things; others have spoken of the need to fight only "necessary" not "unnecessary" wars;

in the past people have argued for fighting only for "vital" national interests in "core" areas and avoiding fights in the "periphery." The problem with all of these sensible-sounding proposals is that it is often only in hindsight that we can be sure what was "stupid" and what was "necessary," what was "vital" and what was "peripheral" and safely ignored.

There were many smart people who believed that American intervention in Vietnam was essential to forestall a communist victory, that it was a vital strategic interest for the United States, partly to protect Japan and partly in the overall effort to resist aggression. An equally long and distinguished list of foreign policy thinkers and politicians supported the war in Iraq because they believed it was vital to protect the world from what most believed were Iraq's WMD programs and from a serial aggressor and mass killer. Later on, when those efforts failed, when the intelligence proved faulty and the political-military strategies inadequate, many of those who supported those wars declared not only that they were a mistake but they were an obvious and avoidable mistake— even though they themselves did not see it at the time. That is one of the problems: many mistakes are not obvious until they are made. So, too, the distinction between supposedly "necessary" and "unnecessary" wars. Prior to December 1941 and Germany's declaration of war on the United States, many American experts and the great majority of the American people did not think it was necessary to go to war in Europe to defeat Hitler.

As for wars on the periphery, the world is not a collection of distinct regions neatly walled off from one another. We may call one region "Europe," one "Asia," and one "the Middle East," and we may say we will intervene in one but not the other. This is an artificial construct, however. Regions abut one another and bleed into one another; their histories, cultures, and religions as well as their economies are tightly entangled. Great powers have been intervening in the Middle East and Persian Gulf for centuries, before there was oil and before there was a Suez Canal. To extricate ourselves from the Middle East would mean extricating ourselves from the world connected to and through the whole region. Even that might not keep us from having to intervene. In recent decades we have learned, tragically, that what happens in the Middle East does not stay in the Middle East. Americans would love never to have to think about the Middle East again, but no administration has succeeded in extricating the United States from it—not even Obama. Meanwhile, the more we rely on proxies like Saudi Arabia, Egypt, and Israel to determine the course of events in the Middle East, the less it will be a course we would choose. Even if they could manage the task without us, which seems unlikely, it will be their interests they will be protecting, not ours, and not those of the liberal order.

For the United States, it is not a question of all in or all out. We cannot intervene everywhere, and we haven't ever come close to doing so. In the Middle East and elsewhere, we will still be required to make decisions: when to intervene, how to intervene, how much to commit, and how long to stay, and the answers will not be obvious and the outcomes will not be certain or even predictable. Nor will our interventions "solve" the problem; or they will solve one problem and create others. Those who insist on outcomes that pose no further dangers and require no further involvement are asking the impossible. Our intervention in World War II defeated Hitler but led to Soviet communist control of half of Europe and four decades of Cold War. That is the messy reality. President Obama said he didn't like the idea of just putting a lid on problems like Syria. But the most masterful foreign policies in history, whether those of a Bismarck or a Disraeli, have always been about containing rather than solving problems. America's entire grand strategy since World War II has been about putting lids on problems, in Europe, in Asia, and elsewhere. Whether that is good or bad depends on what's under the lid and whether it is better to keep things under it than to let them out.

The American people would like a foreign policy that avoids mistakes and disasters, and who can blame them? But that is a bit like wanting to throw touchdowns but not interceptions, to make only good investment decisions, or to win all your cases. The price of failures in foreign policy is measured in human lives and national treasure, and therefore the greatest care must be taken to get it right, but it nevertheless remains a human activity and therefore subject both to our foibles and the failure of our best-intentioned efforts to predict the future. People don't stop what they're doing after a mistake is made; they try to do a better job next time. We can't quit having a foreign policy, even if our geography, our wealth, and our power sorely tempt us to try.

There are, moreover, two kinds of errors: errors of commission and errors of omission. After World War I, Americans were more focused on the former; after World War II, they worried more about the latter. Today we are fixated almost entirely on errors of commission. A couple of years ago, Robert Merry, the editor of *The American Conservative*, made a list of "America's Five Biggest Foreign Policy Fiascoes." At the top of the list was Iraq, followed by America's entry into World

War I, the Vietnam War, the intervention in Somalia, and the Bay of Pigs "invasion." These were all acts of commission. But what about the "fiascoes" that resulted from our failure to act? What about our failure to destroy al Qaeda bases in Afghanistan before three thousand people were killed in the Twin Towers and the Pentagon; or the failure either to deter or to prepare adequately for a Japanese attack on the Philippines, which led in early 1942 to the death of ten thousand American and Filipino soldiers in three months of fighting followed by the deaths of thousands more in the infamous Bataan Death March? Was that not a far worse error than the tragedy which led to eighteen American dead in Mogadishu? What about the price the liberal world order, and particularly America's key allies in Europe, have paid for our failure to contain the crisis in Syria? Were not these errors of omission more costly than our errors of commission in Somalia?

At the root of such thinking is the belief that there is an escape from power or that it is possible to wield power without error and without failure. Americans, blessed by their favorable geography and wealth, still believe they have a choice between engaging the world and letting the world fend for itself. There has been no shortage of realists, idealists, progressives, and conservatives telling them that substantially disengaging from our alliances and overseas commitments is possible and cost-free. But the real choice we face is not between the good and the bad but between the bad and the worse. It is between maintaining the liberal world order, with all the moral and material costs that entails, or letting it collapse and courting the catastrophes that must inevitably follow.

What is likely to follow is a return to the multipolar power struggles that brought so much devastation to the world before the United States redirected the course of history. That is where the deep ruts lead, back to the state of the world prior to 1945. Only this time, the powers competing and clashing will be armed with nuclear weapons. It is ironic that some of those who spent the Cold War warning that America's hawkish foreign policies would result in nuclear holocaust do not seem to fear nuclear war in the competitive multipolar world that may be our future. We have yet to test the question of whether nations with nuclear weapons can go to war, because so far the United States and the liberal world order have prevented such wars. But if history is any guide, to count on the horror of new weaponry alone to maintain the peace is a most risky bet. Had you cast that bet before the two world wars, you would have lost. These days some experts tell us it was the existence of nuclear weapons that prevented the United States and the Soviet Union from coming to blows, but few at the time had any confidence that nuclear weapons were a guarantor of peace. Throughout much of the Cold War there were those who simply assumed that the world was heading inevitably toward Armageddon. They were wrong that it would come as a result of American Cold War policies, but in the long run they may still prove right.

These are the quandaries we cannot avoid no matter how hard we try. Reinhold Niebuhr believed that what he called "the world problem" could not be solved if America did not "accept its full share of responsibility in solving it."[187] To support a "world community beyond our own borders" he went on, both was virtuous and reflected a "prudent understanding of our own interests." But he also predicted that Americans would be "the poorer for the global responsibilities which we bear." And poorer not just in a material sense but also in a moral sense. It was impossible "to build a community without the manipulation of power," and it was impossible "to use power and remain completely 'pure.'"[188] As Hans Morgenthau put it, "Whoever wants to retain his moral innocence must forsake action altogether." Niebuhr did not want Americans to have an "easy conscience" about the things they were going to have to do, for there was always the danger that they would enjoy power too much and would use it to dominate others rather than to address the "world problem." But he also did not want their "uneasy conscience" to "tempt us into irresponsibility."[189]

Americans, it is fair to say, have not enjoyed power too much. These days, they would prefer to wield it less. Yet the struggle for power in the international system is eternal, and so is the struggle over beliefs and ideals. If it is not our system of security and our beliefs shaping the world order, it will be someone else's. If we do not preserve the liberal order, it will be replaced by another kind of order, or more likely by disorder and chaos of the kind we saw in the twentieth century. That is what the world "as it is" looks like. That is what history and human nature have led to in the past and will lead to in the future if not continually shaped, managed, and resisted.

This is a pessimistic view of human existence, but it is not a fatalistic view. Nothing is determined, not the triumph of liberalism nor its defeat. As we have seen these past seventy-five years, even in a dangerous world tremendous human progress and human betterment are possible. The "better angels" of human nature can be encouraged and the demons dampened.

To know that the jungle will always be there is not to despair of keeping it at bay, as we have done for decades. In 1956 the German American historian Fritz Stern wrote that "the deepening of our historical experiences" should not lead us to abandon our faith in "the possibilities of human progress" but rather to "a stronger sense of the precariousness of human freedom and to a still greater dedication to it."[190] The liberal order is as precarious as it is precious. It is a garden that needs constant tending lest the jungle grow back and engulf us all.

ACKNOWLEDGMENTS

This book grew out of an essay written for *Idea,* a magazine conceived and edited by Leon Wieseltier which unfortunately never appeared. I am grateful for the generous support of Roger Hertog and the Hertog Foundation, Stephen and Barbara Friedman, and the Brookings Foreign Policy Leadership Council. Hal Brands, Melvyn Leffler, Will Moreland, Michael O'Hanlon, Gary Schmitt, Strobe Talbott, and Leon Wieseltier read early drafts, and I am most grateful for their many insights and suggestions. My other astute readers were my children, Elena and David, and, as always, my wife, Toria. And, of course, my father, Donald Kagan, to whom this book is dedicated.

NOTES

1. The one exception was the conflict between American and Chinese troops in Korea in 1950–1951.
2. See Steven Pinker, *The Better Angels of Our Nature: Why Violence Has Declined* (New York, 2011).
3. Georg Wilhelm Friedrich Hegel, *The Philosophy of History* (New York, 1956), 19; Francis Fukuyama, *The End of History and the Last Man* (New York, 1992), 48.
4. Ronald Steel, *Walter Lippmann and the American Century* (Boston, 1980), 375.
5. Hannah Arendt, *The Origins of Totalitarianism* (New York, 1951), ix.
6. Judith N. Shklar, *After Utopia: The Decline of Political Faith* (1957; Princeton, NJ, 2015), vii.
7. Arendt, *The Origins of Totalitarianism,* ix.
8. G. John Ikenberry, "The Rise of China and Future of the West: Can the Liberal System Survive?" *Foreign Affairs* 87, no. 1 (January/February 2008); Oona A. Hathaway and Scott J. Schapiro, *The Internationalists* (New York, 2017), xiv; Pinker, *The Better Angels of Our Nature,* 180.
9. Walter Russell Mead, "A Debate on America's Role—25 Years Late," *Wall Street Journal,* May 22, 2017.
10. Speech by President Barack Obama, June 23, 2011.
11. Pew Research Center, May 4, 2016, http://www.people-press.org/2016/05/05/public-uncertain-divided-over-americas-place-in-the-world/; accessed March 6, 2018.

12. Kendrick A. Clements, *William Jennings Bryan: Missionary Isolationist* (Knoxville, TN, 1982), 11.

13. Norman Angell, *The Great Illusion* (2009; New York, 2010), 317.

14. "The Defense of the Atlantic World," *The New Republic*, February 17, 1917.

15. Wolfgang J. Mommsen, *Imperial Germany, 1867–1918: Politics, Culture, and Society in an Authoritarian State* (1995; London, 2009), 209.

16. Heinrich August Winkler, *Age of Catastrophe: A History of the West 1914–1945*, trans. Stewart Spencer (New Haven, CT, 2015), 10.

17. Mommsen, *Imperial Germany*, 209–10.

18. Steel, *Walter Lippmann and the American Century*, 110–12.

19. Ezra Pound, *Hugh Selwyn Mauberley*, 1920.

20. Henry L. Stimson, *On Active Service in Peace and War* (1947; New York, 1948), 305–7.

21. Ibid.

22. James T. Patterson, *Mr. Republican: A Biography of Robert A. Taft* (Boston, 1972), 198.

23. Hans J. Morgenthau, "The Mainsprings of American Foreign Policy: The National Interest vs. Moral Abstractions," *American Political Science Review* 44, no. 4 (December 1950): 850.

24. Lynne Olson, *Those Angry Days: Roosevelt, Lindbergh, and America's Fight over World War II, 1939–1941* (New York, 2013), 222–24.

25. Franklin Delano Roosevelt address at the University of Virginia, June 10, 1940, http://www.presidency.ucsb.edu/ws/?pid=15965#ixzz2glEu6Ehs.

26. Patterson, *Mr. Republican*, 198–99.

27. Howard K. Beale, "Some Fallacies of the Interventionist View" (Washington, DC, 1941), https://babel.hathitrust.org/cgi/pt?id=wu.89095842324;view=1up;seq=3.

28. Robert A. Taft radio address, July 15, 1941, in Clarence E. Wunderlin, Jr., ed., *The Papers of Robert A. Taft*, Vol. 2: *1939–1944* (Kent, OH, 2001), 266; Beale, "Some Fallacies of the Interventionist View"; A. J. Muste quoted in Justus D. Doenecke, *The Battle Against Intervention, 1939–1941* (Malabar, FL, 1997), 25.

29. Paul Kennedy, *The Rise and Fall of the Great Powers: Economic Change and Military Conflict from 1500 to 2000* (New York, 1987), 155.

30. John Darwin, *Unfinished Empire: The Global Expansion of Britain* (New York, 2012), 401.

31. Edward Grey, 1st Viscount Grey of Fallodon, *Twenty-Five Years, 1892–1916* (New York, 1925), Vol. II, 147–48; Theodore Roosevelt, "The International Posse Comitatus," *New York Times*, November 8, 1914.

32. *The New Republic*, February 17, 1917.

33. Today all the available evidence suggests that Hitler intended eventually to go to war with the United States whenever a favorable moment presented itself. As far back as the late 1920s he had been "clear in his own mind that Germany deserved to conquer the globe." Gerhard Weinberg, *Visions of Victory* (New York, 2005), 8, 15. Hitler revealed his thinking in 1928 in what is known as his "Second Book," the unpublished sequel to *Mein Kampf.* He had originally expected to leave the task to a next generation of successors, but in 1940 and 1941, after the easy and rapid successes in the West and what he anticipated would be an equally rapid defeat of the Soviet Union, his timetable accelerated. Once the conquest of Russia had been achieved, his plan was to shift German industrial production from supporting the army to building the ships and planes necessary to take on both the British and the Americans. In July 1941, with the eastern conflict apparently going well, Hitler began preparing for war with the United States. Plans were drawn up "for the establishment of an Atlantic power base embracing the Near East, North-west Africa, territories for colonial expansion and overseas support bases." Once that was established, Germany would build a "big battleship navy," perhaps including remnants of the defeated or co-opted British fleet, to use against the United States. Klaus Hildebrand, *The Foreign Policy of the Third Reich*, trans. Anthony Fothergill (1970; Berkeley, CA, 1973), 113. The anti-interventionists claimed that an amphibious invasion across open oceans against a heavily defended coast was impossible. But as subsequent events would show, the massive, complex, and immensely difficult operation that *The New York Times*'s military editor, Hanson Baldwin, described was precisely the kind of attack the United States and Great Britain eventually launched against the Germans on D-Day. Hanson W. Baldwin, *United We Stand! Defense of the Western Hemisphere* (New

York, 1941), 78–79. It is not impossible to imagine that Hitler, having defeated all the other enemies on the Eurasian continent, having gained control of their industrial capacities and populations, and having destroyed or captured the British navy, would next have sought to neutralize American naval power and then attempted the same kind of operation. Gerhard Weinberg, *A World At Arms: A Global History of World War II* (New York, 1994), 204–5.

34. Robert L Beisner, *Dean Acheson: A Life in the Cold War* (New York, 2006), 13–14, 21–22.

35. Melvyn P. Leffler, *A Preponderance of Power: National Security, the Truman Administration, and the Cold War* (Palo Alto, CA, 1993), 56.

36. Robert A. Divine, *Second Chance: The Triumph of Internationalism in America During World War II* (New York, 1967), 84.

37. Beisner, *Dean Acheson*, 151–52, 156.

38. Ibid., 13–14, 21–22.

39. John W. Dower, *Japan in War and Peace: Selected Essays* (New York, 1995), 165.

40. David McCullough, *Truman* (New York, 1992), 234.

41. Senator Burton Wheeler, for instance, insisted it was tantamount to saying "To hell with the United States." Divine, *Second Chance*, 152.

42. Ibid., 159. Even future Cold Warriors like Truman and Acheson did not yet view the Soviets as a likely adversary.

43. As the Cold War historian John Lewis Gaddis has noted, Roosevelt and his advisers wanted to protect the United States against any dangers that might arise, but "they lacked a clear sense of what those might be or where they might arise. Their thinking about postwar security was, as a consequence, more general than specific." John Lewis Gaddis, *We Now Know: Rethinking Cold War History* (Oxford, UK, 1997), 12.

44. President Franklin D. Roosevelt fireside chat, December 24, 1943, http://www.presidency.ucsb.edu/ws/index.php?pid=16356.

45. Beisner, *Dean Acheson*, 52, 530, 373.

46. Ron Chernow, *Alexander Hamilton* (New York, 2004), 60.

47. http://tenthamendmentcenter.com/historical-documents/federalist -papers/federalist-10-the-same-subject-continued-the-union-as-a -safeguard-against-domestic-faction-and-insurrection/.

48. As the progressive journalist Freda Kirchwey put it, the "alternative to an unsatisfactory international order," it turned out, had not been "a satisfactory international order" but "uncontrolled power politics" and "international anarchy." Elizabeth Borgwardt, *A New Deal for the World* (Cambridge, MA, 2007),171.

49. Robert Dallek, *Franklin Roosevelt and American Foreign Policy, 1932–1945* (Oxford, UK, 1979), 506.

50. Even before the First World War, British officials had privately regarded the empire as a "gouty giant" held together chiefly by bluff. Michael Howard, *The Continental Commitment: The Dilemma of British Defence Policy in the Era of the Two World Wars* (London, 1972), 75.

51. Marc Trachtenberg, *A Constructed Peace: The Making of the European Settlement, 1945–1963* (Princeton, NJ, 1999), 85.

52. See Dower, *Japan in War and Peace,* 155–61.

53. Dennis L. Bark and David R. Gress, *A History of Western Germany,* Vol. 1: *From Shadow to Substance, 1945–1963* (Hoboken, NJ, 1989), 86.

54. Dower, *Japan in War and Peace,* 166, 169, 27.

55. Bark and Gress, *A History of Western Germany,* 177.

56. Dower, *Japan in War and Peace,* 15, 24–26, 173.

57. See Robert Gilpin, "The Theory of Hegemonic War," *Journal of Interdisciplinary History* 18, no. 4 (Spring 1988): 591–613.

58. G. John Ikenberry, *After Victory: Institutions, Strategic Restraint, and the Rebuilding of Order After Major Wars* (Princeton, NJ, 2000), 186.

59. On this point, see Ronald Hyam, *Britain's Declining Empire: The Road to Decolonisation, 1918–1968* (Cambridge, UK, 2006).

60. Giovanni Arrighi, "The World Economy and the Cold War, 1970–1990," in Melvyn P. Leffler and Odd Arne Westad, *The Cambridge History of the Cold War,* Vol. III: *Endings* (2010; Cambridge, UK, 2011), 26.

61. Wilfried Loth, "The Cold War and the Social and Economic History of the Twentieth Century," in Leffler and Westad, *The Cambridge History of the Cold War,* Vol. II: *Crises and Détente* (2010; Cambridge, UK, 2011), 512.

62. Arrighi, "The World Economy and the Cold War, 1970–1990," 26.

63. Left behind were Latin America and sub-Saharan Africa. Ibid., 36.

64. Ibid., 41.

65. Ikenberry, *After Victory,* 190.

66. Gaddis, *We Now Know,* 43–44.

67. For examples of American willingness to override or disregard allied views throughout the Cold War and beyond, see Stephen Sestanovich, *Maximalist: America in the World from Truman to Obama* (New York, 2014).

68. This option was not as readily available to Japan, given its "peace constitution" and American control of its defense policies. But in any case, the Japanese people were not interested in more military spending, even when American policymakers would have preferred it.

69. Odd Arne Westad, *The Cold War: A World History* (New York, 2017), 3.

70. Geir Lundestad, *The United States and Western Europe Since 1945* (New York, 2005), 37.

71. For extensive evidence of the link between the Cold War and civil rights, see Mary L. Dudziak, *Cold War Civil Rights: Race and the Image of American Democracy* (Princeton, NJ, 2000).

72. Address by Richard M. Nixon to the Bohemian Club, San Francisco, July 29, 1967.

73. For an advocate of the Reagan approach, see Elliott Abrams, *Realism and Democracy: American Foreign Policy After the Arab Spring* (New York, 2017).

74. Samuel P. Huntington, *The Third Wave: Democratization in the Late Twentieth Century* (Norman, OK, 1991), 98.

75. Even in the United States insecurity led to the federal Constitution, replacing the looser Articles of Confederation, and individual rights have been abridged most at times of real or perceived insecurity.

76. That Stalin's economic plans would lead to massive economic failure would not become clear to outside observers until after the war.

77. Loth, "The Cold War and the Social and Economic History of the Twentieth Century," 504–5.

78. Ibid., 506.

79. George Kennan to George Marshall ["Long Telegram"], February 22, 1946, Harry S. Truman Administration File, Elsey Papers, Harry S. Truman Presidential Library and Museum; https://www.trumanlibrary.org/whistlestop/study_collections/coldwar/documents/pdf/6-6.pdf.

80. As Kennan observed, "there was a time when the Communist Party represented far more of a minority in the sphere of Russian national life than Soviet power today represents in the world community." Ibid.

81. John Mueller, "Questing for Monsters to Destroy," in Melvyn P. Leffler and Jeffrey W. Legro, eds., *In Uncertain Times: American Foreign Policy After the Berlin Wall and 9/11* (Ithaca, NY, 2011), 117.

82. Hyam, *Britain's Declining Empire*, 302.

83. Franklin Roosevelt certainly believed the United States would be able to work with the Soviet Union as an international partner after the war, as did most of the important officials and most members of Congress. On Acheson's change of perspective, for instance, see Beisner, *Dean Acheson*, 28–47.

84. Loth, "The Cold War and the Social and Economic History of the Twentieth Century," 510.

85. George Kennan to George Marshall ["Long Telegram"], February 22, 1946.

86. Although Kennan and the authors of NSC-68 differed on many points, and Kennan would oppose the recommendations of the later document, they did not disagree about this.

87. William Taubman, *Gorbachev: His Life and Times* (New York, 2017), 263.

88. Ibid., 245. Reagan in their eyes had ended détente, abandoned arms control, tried to divide the Soviet bloc, and resisted Soviet influence throughout the world by arming anticommunist insurgencies in Nicaragua, Cambodia, Angola, and Afghanistan. He had threatened an arms race in space and called the Soviet Union an "evil empire." Ibid., 275.

89. Sestanovich, *Maximalist*, 240.

90. Arrighi, "The World Economy and the Cold War, 1970–1990," 28, 37–38.

91. In 1961, the old Bolshevik Anastas Mikoyan declared that the two Germanys were the place where it would be determined whether or not Marxism-Leninism was "right" and communism was "the higher, better form of social organization," and that if it did not triumph in East Germany then "we have not triumphed." Loth, "The Cold War and the Social and Economic History of the Twentieth Century," 517.

92. Ibid., 523.

93. Taubman, *Gorbachev*, 266.

94. Trachtenberg, *A Constructed Peace*, 64

95. The brief crackdown in Lithuania by Russian forces was an exception, but it was minor compared to what any serious effort would have entailed.

96. Taubman, *Gorbachev*, 263.

97. Trachtenberg, *A Constructed Peace*, 401–2.

98. K. O. Morgan, cited in Hyam, *Britain's Declining Empire*, 404.

99. Mueller, "Questing for Monsters to Destroy," 128.

100. Walter Lippmann, *The Cold War: A Study in U.S. Foreign Policy* (New York, 1947), 10, 18, 20, 22.

101. Connie Sachs in John le Carré's *Smiley's People* (New York, 1979).

102. Reinhold Niebuhr, *The Irony of American History* (New York, 1952), 4.

103. Lewis Sorley, *A Better War: The Unexamined Victories and Final Tragedy of America's Last Years in Vietnam* (New York 1999), 386.

104. Ibid., 20.

105. Noam Chomsky, *American Power and the New Mandarins: Historical and Political Essays* (New York, 1969), 316.

106. Address by Secretary of State Henry Kissinger to the Commonwealth Club of San Francisco, February 3, 1976.

107. Statement by Secretary of State Henry Kissinger before the Senate Foreign Relations Committee, September 19, 1974; https://history .state.gov/historicaldocuments/frus1969-76v38p1/d45.

108. Richard Nixon, interview by Hedley Donovan, Henry Grunwald, Hugh Sidey, and Jerrold Schecter, *Time*, January 3, 1972.

109. Sestanovich, *Maximalist*, 178.

110. Lundestad, *The United States and Western Europe Since 1945*, 249; emphasis in original.

111. See ibid.

112. *The Times* of London, the *Frankfurter Rundschau*, and *Libération*. Robert Kagan, "The Ambivalent Superpower," *Politico*, February 27, 2014.

113. Beisner, *Dean Acheson*, 373.

114. Sestanovich, *Maximalist*, 170.

115. Brent Scowcroft and George H. W. Bush, *A World Transformed* (New York, 1998), 322.

116. Ibid., 340.

117. George Will, "Panama: A Moment for Bush to Savor a Good-neighbor Policy with Best of Intentions," *Orlando Sentinel,* December 22, 1989.

118. David Halberstam, *War in a Time of Peace: Bush, Clinton, and the Generals* (New York, 2001), 326.

119. Ted R. Bromund, Michael Auslin, and Colin Dueck, "Reclaiming American Realism," *American Affairs* 1, no. 2 (Summer 2017); Walter Russell Mead, "Trump Brings Foreign Policy Back to Earth," *Wall Street Journal,* November 29, 2017.

120. Sestanovich, *Maximalist,* 244.

121. Ralf Dahrendorf, *Reflections on the Revolution in Europe* (New York, 1990), 120.

122. Lundestad, *The United States and Western Europe Since 1945,* 234.

123. Hans J. Morgenthau, "The Mainsprings of American Foreign Policy: The National Interest vs. Moral Abstractions," *American Political Science Review* 44, no. 4 (December 1950): 838.

124. Francis Fukuyama, "The End of History," *The National Interest* 16 (Summer 1989): 16, 17.

125. For a look back at the controversy surrounding this document, see Eric S. Edelman, "The Strange Career of the 1992 Defense Planning Guidance," in Leffler and Legro, *In Uncertain Times,* 74. The Huntington quotation is also on p. 74.

126. Patrick Tyler, "U.S. Strategy Plan Calls for Insuring No Rivals Develop," *New York Times,* March 8, 1992.

127. Jeane Kirkpatrick, "A Normal Country in a Normal Time," *The National Interest* 21 (Fall 1990): 40–45.

128. Derek Chollet and James Goldgeier, *America Between the Wars: From 11/9 to 9/11* (New York, 2008), 209.

129. After the al Qaeda attacks on the American embassies in Kenya and Tanzania killed two hundred in 1998, Clinton ordered cruise missile strikes on al Qaeda's camps and on a suspected chemical factory in Sudan—and was criticized by Republicans for doing so. But the only reliable way of eliminating the al Qaeda bases would have involved

a large-scale and long-term operation in Afghanistan, and as officials later recalled, that was "almost unthinkable, absent a provocation like 9/11." Ibid., 269.

130. Ibid., 207.

131. Ibid., 247.

132. Ibid., 195–96.

133. Ibid., 197. The Republican leader in the Senate, Trent Lott, announced: "I cannot support military action in the Persian Gulf at this time." Ibid., 201.

134. Sestanovich, *Maximalist,* 285.

135. Al Gore speech to the Council on Foreign Relations, February 12, 2002, http://p2004.org/gore/goreo21202t.html.

136. Speech on Senate floor by Senator Hillary Clinton, October 10, 2002.

137. After weapons investigators discovered none of the suspected caches of chemical, biological, and nuclear weapons materials, a *Washington Post*/ABC News poll in April 2003 found that, nevertheless, over 70 percent of Americans supported the war, and a CBS poll revealed that 60 percent of Americans believed it had been "the right thing to do." A month later, a Gallup poll found that 72 percent of Americans still supported the war. *Washington Post*/ABC News, "Poll: Iraq War," April 4, 2003, http://www.washingtonpost.com/wp-srv/politics/polls/vault/stories/data040303.htm; Lloyd Vries, "Poll: U.S. Backs Bush on War," CBS News, March 21, 2003, https://www.cbsnews.com/news/poll-us-backs-bush-on-war/; Frank Newport, "Seventy-Two Percent of Americans Support War Against Iraq," Gallup, March 24, 2003, http://news.gallup.com/poll/8038/seventytwo-percent-americans-support-war-against-iraq.aspx.

138. "America's Forever Wars," *New York Times,* October 23, 2017, A20.

139. Masha Gessen, *The Future Is History: How Totalitarianism Reclaimed Russia* (New York, 2017), 116, 197, 233.

140. Lilia Shevtsova, *Lonely Power: Why Russia Has Failed to Become the West and the West Is Weary of Russia* (Washington, DC, 2010), 144.

141. James Kirchick, *The End of Europe: Dictators, Demagogues, and the Coming Dark Age* (New Haven, CT, 2018), 22.

142. As the Russia scholar Leon Aron has noted, "modern Russian history is replete with examples of regime change in the wake of a foreign-

policy or military setback." Leon Aron, "What Is Putinism?" *Journal of Democracy* 28, no. 4 (October 2017): 79.

143. David Shambaugh, *China Goes Global: The Partial Power* (New York, 2013), 29.

144. Ibid., 32, 34, 20.

145. Xi Jinping speech delivered at the 19th National Congress of the Communist Party of China, October 18, 2017.

146. William Jefferson Clinton address, "On China and the National Interest," Washington, DC, October 24, 1997.

147. See Kurt M. Campbell and Ely Ratner, "The China Reckoning." *Foreign Affairs* 92, no. 2 (March/April 2018).

148. Catherine Wallace, "Japanese Nationalism Today: Risky Resurgence, Necessary Evil or New Normal?" *Mejiro Journal of Humanities*, no. 12 (March 2016): 69.

149. "The mounting tension centered on war memory politics today among Japan, China, and the Koreas is not only about righting past wrongs, but also about jockeying for position in the shifting geopolitics owing largely to the rise of China, and the continuing belligerence of North Korea as well as Japan's own foreign policy under the Abe administration." Akiko Hashimoto, "Nationalism, Pacifism, and Reconciliation: Three Paths Forward for Japan's 'History Problem,'" *The Asia-Pacific Journal* (October 25, 2016): 10.

150. Wallace, "Japanese Nationalism Today," 73.

151. Ibid., 74.

152. Mark Leonard, *Why Europe Will Run the 21st Century* (New York, 2005); Niall Ferguson, "Dense Fog in the Channel," *Boston Globe*, May 30, 2016.

153. Lundestad, *The United States and Western Europe Since 1945*, 235.

154. Sestanovich, *Maximalist*, 247.

155. Michael Howard quoted in Dahrendorf, *Reflections on the Revolution in Europe*, 153.

156. Dahrendorf, *Reflections on the Revolution in Europe*, 123.

157. Christoph Bertram, "The German Question," *Foreign Affairs* 69, no. 2 (Spring 1990).

158. Helmut Schmidt speech to the German Social Democratic Party conference, December 4, 2011; http://library.fes.de/pdf-files/id/ipa/08888.pdf.

159. Thomas Mann address to the Library of Congress, "Germany and the Germans," May 29, 1945.

160. Ivan Krastev, *After Europe*, 10.

161. "Europe's Populists Are Waltzing into the Mainstream," *The Economist*, February 3, 2018.

162. Krastev, *After Europe*, 63.

163. Arendt, *The Origins of Totalitarianism*, 263.

164. Ira Katznelson, *Desolation and Enlightenment: Political Knowledge After Total War, Totalitarianism, and the Holocaust* (New York, 2004), 14.

165. Ibid., 15.

166. Krastev, *After Europe*, 18.

167. Timothy Garton Ash, "It's the Kultur, Stupid," *New York Review of Books*, December 7, 2017.

168. Reuters "Obama Says U.S. Military Strikes Could Not Have Stopped Syria Misery," March 29, 2014; https://www.reuters.com/article/us-syria-crisis-obama/obama-says-u-s-military-strikes-could-not-have-stopped-syria-misery-idUSBREA2R21O20140329.

169. Krastev, *After Europe*, 13–14.

170. Thomas Wright, *All Measures Short of War: The Contest for the Twenty-first Century and the Future of American Power* (New Haven, CT, 2017), 63.

171. Viktor Orbán speech at the Bálványos Free Summer University and Youth Camp, July 26, 2014.

172. Fareed Zakaria, *The Post-American World* (New York, 2008); Wright, *All Measures Short of War*, 39.

173. H. R. McMaster and Gary D. Cohn, "America First Doesn't Mean America Alone," *Wall Street Journal*, May 30, 2017.

174. Daniel W. Drezner, "The Most Extraordinary Op-ed of 2017," *Washington Post*, June 1, 2017.

175. Sean Wilentz, "Fighting Words," *The World News*, March 19, 2018; Dahrendorf, *Reflections on the Revolution in Europe*, 5.

176. Patrick J. Buchanan, *A Republic, Not an Empire* (Washington, DC, 1999); Patrick Henry quoted in Jonathan Marshall, "Empire or Liberty: The Anti-Federalists and Foreign Policy, 1787–1788," *Journal of Libertarian Studies* 4, no. 3 (Summer 1980): 248–49.

177. Doenecke, *The Battle Against Intervention*, 68.
178. Samuel P. Huntington, *Who Are We? The Challenges to American National Identity* (New York, 2004), 310–16.
179. David French, "Donald Trump Struck a Righteous Blow Against Universalism," *National Review*, July 7, 2017.
180. Krastev, *After Europe*, 6.
181. Erich Fromm, *The Anatomy of Human Destructiveness* (New York, 1973), 20, 31.
182. Isaiah Berlin, "Counter-Enlightenment," in Isaiah Berlin, *Against the Current: Essays in the History of Ideas* (Princeton, NJ, 1979), 16–18, 28–29.
183. Reuters, "China State Media Attacks Western Democracy Ahead of Congress," October 17, 2017; https://www.reuters.com/article/us-china-congress-politics/china-state-media-attacks-western-democracy-ahead-of-congress-idUSKBN1CM0AB.
184. Eric Hobsbawm, *The Age of Extremes, 1914–1991* (New York, 1995), 112; Katznelson, *Desolation and Enlightenment*, 15.
185. M. Steven Fish, "What Is Putinism?" *Journal of Democracy* 28, no. 4 (October 2017): 64.
186. Ibid.
187. Reinhold Niebuhr, "Christianity and Crisis," in D. B. Robertson, *Love and Justice: Selections from the Shorter Writings of Reinhold Niebuhr* (Louisville, KY, 1957), 200.
188. Reinhold Niebuhr, *The Irony of American History* (Chicago, 1952), 4.
189. Ibid., 7; Robertson, *Love and Justice*, 205.
190. Fritz Stern, "Introduction," in Fritz Stern, ed., *The Varieties of History* (New York, 1956), 24; Katznelson, *Desolation and Enlightenment*, 2.

THE WORLD AMERICA MADE

Upon its initial publication, *The World America Made* became one of the most talked about political books of the year, influencing Barack Obama's 2012 State of the Union address and shaping the thought of both the Obama and Romney presidential campaigns. In these incisive and engaging pages, Kagan responds to those who anticipate— or even long for—a post-American world order by showing what a decline in America's influence would truly mean for the United States and the rest of the world as the vital institutions, economies, and ideals currently supported by American power wane or disappear. As Kagan notes, it has happened before: one need only to consider the consequences of the breakdown of the Roman Empire and the collapse of the European order during World War I. This book is a powerful warning that America need not and dare not decline by committing preemptive superpower suicide.

Political Science

DANGEROUS NATION

*America's Foreign Policy from Its Earliest Days
to the Dawn of the Twentieth Century*

Most Americans believe the United States had been an isolationist power until the twentieth century. This is wrong. In a riveting and brilliantly revisionist work of history, Robert Kagan shows how Americans have, in fact, been steadily increasing their global power and influence from the beginning. Driven by commercial, territorial, and idealistic ambitions, the United States has always perceived itself, and has been seen by other nations, as an international force. *Dangerous Nation* is of great importance to our understanding of our nation's history and its role in the global community.

History

Hopes for a new peaceful international order after the end of the Cold War have been dashed by sobering realities: Great powers are once again competing for honor and influence. The world remains "unipolar," but international competition among the United States, Russia, China, Europe, Japan, India, and Iran raises new threats of regional conflict, and a new contest between Western liberalism and the great Eastern autocracies of Russia and China has reinjected ideology into geopolitics. For the past few years, the liberal world has been internally divided and distracted by issues both profound and petty. Robert Kagan masterfully poses the most important questions facing the liberal democratic countries, challenging them to choose whether they want to shape history or let others shape it for them.

Current Affairs

ALSO AVAILABLE
Of Paradise and Power